Table of Contents

Introduction

What is Summer Academic Learning Loss?

Studies show that if students take a standardized test at the end of the school year, and then repeat that test when they return in the fall, they will lose approximately four to six weeks of learning. In other words, they could potentially miss more questions in the fall than they would in the spring. This loss is commonly referred to as the summer slide.

When these standardized testing scores drop an average of one month it causes teachers to spend at least the first four to five weeks, on average, re-teaching critical material. In terms of math, students typically lose an average of two and a half months of skills and when reading and math losses are combined, it averages three months; it may even be lower for students in lower income homes.

And on average, the three areas students will typically lose ground in are spelling, vocabulary, and mathematics.

How can You Help Combat Summer Learning Loss?

Like anything, academics are something that requires practice and if they are not used regularly, you run the risk of losing them. Because of this, it is imperative your children work to keep their minds sharp over the summer. There are many ways to keep your children engaged over the summer and we're going to explore some of the most beneficial.

Start with School:

Your best source of information is your child's school. Have a conversation with your child's teacher. Tell them you are interested in working on some academics over the summer and ask what suggestions they might have. Be sure to ask about any areas your child may be struggling in and for a list of books to read over the summer. Also, talk to your child's counselor. They may have recommendations of local summer activities that will relate back to the schools and what your child needs to know. Finally, ask the front office staff for any information on currently existing after school programs (the counselor may also be able to provide this). Although after school programs may end shortly, the organizations running them will often have information on summer camps. Many of these are often free or at a very low cost to you and your family.

Stay Local:

Scour your local area for free or low cost activities and events. Most museums will have dollar days of some kind where you can get money off admission for going a certain day of the week, or a certain time. Zoos will often do the same thing. Take lunch to the park and eat outside, talking about the leaves, flowers, or anything else you can find there. Your child can pick one favorite thing and research it. Attend concerts or shows put on by local artists, musicians, or other vendors.

There are many, many other options available, you just have to explore and find them. The key here is to engage your children. Have them look online with you or search the local newspapers/magazines. Allow them to plan the itinerary, or work with you on it, and when they get back, have them write a journal about the activity. Or, even better, have them write a letter or email to a family member about what they did.

Practice Daily:

Whether the choice is a family activity, experiencing the local environment, or staying academically focused the key is to keep your child engaged every day. That daily practice helps keep students' minds sharp and focused, ensuring they will be able to not only retain the knowledge they have learned, but in many cases begin to move ahead for the next year.

Summer Strategies for Students

Summer is here which brings a time of excitement, relaxation, and fun. School is the last thing on your mind, but that doesn't mean learning has to be on vacation too. In fact, learning is as just as important, and be just as fun (if not more), during the summer months than during the school year.

Did you know that during the summer:

- Students often lose an average of 2 and ½ months of math skills
- Students often lose 2 months of reading skills
- Teachers spend at least the first 4 to 5 weeks of the next school year reteaching important skills and concepts

Your brain is like a muscle, and like any muscle, it must be worked out regularly, and like this, your language arts and math skills are something that requires practice; if you do not use them regularly, you run the risk of losing them. So, it is very important you keep working through the summer. But, it doesn't always have to be 'school' type work. There are many ways to stay engaged, and we're going to spend a little time looking through them.

Read and Write as Often as Possible

Reading is one of the most important things you can do to keep your brain sharp and engaged. Here are some tips to remember about summer reading:

- Often, summer is the perfect time to find and read new books or books you have always been curious about. However, without your teacher, you may struggle with finding a book that is appropriate for your reading level. In this case, you just have to remember the five finger rule: open a book to a random page and begin reading aloud, holding up one finger for each word you cannot say or do not know. If you have more than five fingers visible, the book is probably too hard.

- Reading goes beyond books; there are so many other ways to read. Magazines are a great way to keep kids connected to learning, and they encourage so many different activities. National Geographic Kids, Ranger Rick, and American Girl are just a few examples. As silly as it may sound, you can also read the backs of cereal boxes and billboards to work on reading confidence and fluency, and learn many new things along the way! And thinking completely outside the box, you can also read when singing karaoke. Reading the words as they flash across the screen is a great way to build fluency. You can also turn the closed captioning on when a TV show is on to encourage literacy and reading fluency.

But writing is equally as important, and there are many things you can do to write over the summer:

- First, consider keeping a journal of your summer activities. You can detail the things you do, places you go, even people you meet. Be sure to include as much description as possible – sights, sounds, colors should all be included so you can easily remember and visualize the images. But the wonderful thing about a journal is that spelling and sentence structure are not as important. It's just the practice of actually writing that is where your focus should be. The other nice thing about a journal is that this informal writing is just for you; with journal writing you don't have to worry about anything, you just want to write.

- But if you want a little more depth to your journaling, and you want to share it with others, there is a fantastic opportunity for you with blogging. With parental approval, you can create a blog online where you can share your summer experiences with friends, family, or any others. The wonderful thing about blogs is that you can play with the privacy settings and choose who you want to see your blogs. You can make it private, where only the individuals who you send the link to can see it, or you can choose for it to be public where anyone can read it. Of course, if you are keeping a blog, you will have to make it a little more formal and pay attention to spelling, grammar, and sentences simply because you want to make sure your blog is pleasing to those who are reading it. Some popular places to post blogs are Blogger, Wordpress, Squarespace, and Quillpad.

Practice Math in Real Life

One way you can keep your brain sharp is by looking at that world around you and finding ways to include math. In this case, we're thinking of fun, practical ways to practice in your daily life.

- First, have some fun this summer with being in charge of some family projects. Suggest a fun project to complete with a parent or grandparent; decide on an area to plant some new bushes or maybe a small home project you can work on together. You can help design the project and maybe even research the best plants to plant or the best way to build the project. Then write the shopping list, making sure you determine the correct amount of supplies you will need. Without even realizing it, you will have used some basic math calculations and geometry to complete the project.

- You can also find math in shopping for groceries or while doing some back to school shopping. For each item that goes into the cart, estimate how much it will be and keep a running estimation of the total cost. Make it a competition before you go by estimating what your total bill will be and see who comes the closest. Or, you can even try and compete to see who can determine the correct total amount of tax that will be needed. And a final mental game to play while shopping is to determine the change you should receive when paying with cash. Not only is this a good skill to practice, it, more importantly, helps you make sure you're getting the correct change.

- You can even use everyday math if you are doing any traveling this summer and there are many fun ways to do this. Traveling requires money, and someone has to be in charge of the budget. You can volunteer to be the family accountant. Make a budget for the trip and keep all the receipts. Tally up the cost of the trip and even try to break it up by category – Food, fun, hotels, gas are just a few of the categories you can include. For those of you that might be looking for even more of a challenge, you can calculate what percentage of your budget has been spent on each category as well.

- And traveling by car gives many opportunities as well. Use the car odometer to calculate how far you have traveled. For an added challenge, you can see if you can calculate how much gas you used as well as how many gallons of gas per mile have been used.

Practice Daily:

Whether the choice is a family activity, experiencing the local environment, or staying academically focused the key is to keep your mind engaged every day. That daily practice helps to keep your brain sharp and focused, and helps ensure you will be able to not only retain the knowledge you learned last year but get a jump start on next year's success too!

How to Use This Workbook Effectively During Summer

This book offers a variety of state standards aligned resources, in both printed and online format, to help students learn during Summer months.

The activities in the book are organized by week and aligned with the 6th-grade learning standards. We encourage you to start at the beginning of Summer holidays. During each week, students can complete daily Math and English practice. There are five daily practice worksheets for each week. Students can log in to the online program once a week to complete reading, vocabulary and writing practice. Students can work on fun activity anytime during that week. Additionally, students can record their Summer activity through the online program.

Please note that online program also includes access to 7th grade learning resources. This section of the online program could be used to help students get a glimpse of what they would be learning in the next grade level.

Participate in the Weekly Competition and Win Prizes!

 Tweet a picture of your Summer fun activity to participate in our exciting weekly competition. It could be a picture of the sandcastle that you built on the beach or your sibling learning to ride a bicycle. Have fun and tweet your picture. Remember to include **@LumosLearning** and **#Summer-Learning**.

Our editors will pick a winner each week and award $50 in Amazon Gift cards!

Take Advantage of the Online Resources

To access the online resources included with this book, parents and teachers can register with a FREE account. With each free signup, student accounts can be associated to enable online access for them. Once the registration is complete, the login credentials for the created accounts will be sent in email to the id used during signup. Students can log in to their student accounts to get started with their summer learning. Parents can use the parent portal to keep track of student's progress.

How to register?

Step 1: Go to the URL or Use the QR code for the signup page
http://www.lumoslearning.com/a/tedbooks

Step 2: Place this book access code
Access Code: G6-7MLSLH-73094

Step 3: Fill in the basic details to complete registration

URL	QR Code
Visit the URL below and place the book access code **http://www.lumoslearning.com/a/tedbooks** **Access Code: G6-7MLSLH-73094**	

Lumos Short Story Competition 2021

**Write a Short Story
Based On Your Summer Experiences**

Get A Chance To Win $100 Cash Prize
+
1 Year Free Subscription To Lumos StepUp
+
Trophy With Certificate

Winner - 2020

Winner - 2019

How can my child participate in this competition?

Step 1
Visit www.lumoslearning.com/a/tedbooks and enter your access code to create Lumos parent account and student account.

Access Code : G6-7MLSLH-73094

Step 2
After registration, your child can upload their summer story by logging into the student portal and clicking on Lumos Short Story Competition 2021.
Last date for submission is August 31, 2021

How is this competition judged?
Lumos teachers will review students submissions in Sep 2021. Quality of submission would be judged based on creativity, coherence and writing skills.

We recommend short stories that are less than 500 words.

Week 1 Summer Practice

Expressing Ratios (6.RP.A.1)

Day 1

1. A school has an enrollment of 600 students. 330 of the students are girls. Express the fraction of students who are boys in simplest terms.

   Ⓐ $\frac{12}{20}$ = $\frac{3}{5}$

   Ⓑ $\frac{11}{20}$ =

   Ⓒ $\frac{9}{20}$

   Ⓓ $\frac{13}{20}$

   $\frac{330}{600}$

   $\begin{array}{r} 119 \\ + 85 \\ \hline 2014 \\ - 45 \\ \hline 159 \end{array}$

2. In the 14th century, the Sultan of Brunei noticed that his ratio of emeralds to rubies was the same as the ratio of diamonds to pearls. If he had 85 emeralds, 119 rubies, and 45 diamonds, how many pearls did he have? 85 em   34

   Ⓐ 17   119R
   Ⓑ 22
   Ⓒ 58
   Ⓓ 63

3. Mr. Fullingham has 75 geese and 125 turkeys. What is the ratio of the number of geese to the total number of birds in simplest terms? 200   3:8

   Ⓐ 75:200   75:125
   Ⓑ 3:8
   Ⓒ 125:200   75:200
   Ⓓ 5:8   G   B

4. Write the ratio that correctly describes the number of white stars compared to the number of gray stars. Write your answer in the box below.

4:5

Day 1

Analysis of Key Events and Ideas (RL.6.1)

As it poured outside, I settled down by the window to watch the rain. The green park opposite my house looked even more green and fresh than usual. Strong winds shook the branches of the tall trees. Some of the branches swayed so hard in the strong winds that I thought they would break.

5. **Why is the author using such clear descriptions?**

   Ⓐ just to say that it was raining hard
   Ⓑ creating imagery to show the reader what that moment was like
   Ⓒ to tell us that the wind was blowing
   Ⓓ to explain what the trees look like when it rains

The Forest's Sentinel

At night, when all is still
The forest's sentinel
Glides silently across the hill
And perches in an old pine tree,
A friendly presence his!
No harm can come
From night bird on the prowl.
His cry is mellow,
Much softer than a peacock's call.
Why then this fear of owls
Calling in the night?
If men must speak,
Then owls must hoot-
They have the right.
On me it casts no spell:
Rather, it seems to cry,
"The night is good- all's well, all's well."
-- RUSKIN BOND

6. **From what point of view is the above poem?**

    (A) First person point of view - from the owl's perspective
    (B) 3rd person point of view - from an unknown bystander or the author
    (C) First person point of view - from another animal's perspective
    (D) None of the above

7. **According to the above poem when does the Owl come out?**

    (A) At night
    (B) At dawn
    (C) At dusk
    (D) At noon

Excerpt from Arabian Nights, Aladdin

After these words, the magician drew a ring off his finger, and put it on one of Aladdin's, telling him that it was a preservative against all evil, while he should observe what he had prescribed to him. After this instruction he said: "Go down boldly, child, and we shall both be rich all our lives."

Aladdin jumped into the cave, descended the steps, and found the three halls just as the African magician had described. He went through them with all the precaution the fear of death could inspire; crossed the garden without stopping, took down the lamp from the niche, threw out the wick and the liquor, and, as the magician had desired, put it in his vestband. But as he came down from the terrace, he stopped in the garden to observe the fruit, which he only had a glimpse of in crossing it. All the trees were loaded with extraordinary fruit, of different colours on each tree. Some bore fruit entirely white, and some clear and transparent as crystal; some pale red, and others deeper; some green, blue, and purple, and others yellow: in short, there were fruits of all colours. The white were pearls; the clear and transparent, diamonds; the deep red, rubies; the green, emeralds; the blue, turquoises; the purple, amethysts; and those that were of yellow cast, sapphires. Aladdin was altogether ignorant of their worth, and would have preferred figs and grapes, or any other fruits. But though he took them only for a coloured glass of little value, yet he was so pleased with the variety of the colours, and the beauty and extraordinary size of the seeming fruit, that he resolved to gather some of every sort; and accordingly filled the two new purses his uncle had bought for him with his clothes. Some he wrapped up in the skirts of his vest, which was of silk, large and full, and he crammed his bosom as full as it could hold.

Aladdin, having thus loaded himself with riches, returned through the three halls with the same precaution, made all the haste he could, that he might not make his uncle wait, and soon arrived at the mouth of the cave, where the African magician expected him with the utmost impatience. As soon as Aladdin saw him, he cried out: "Pray, uncle, lend me your hand, to help me out." "Give me the lamp first," replied the magician; "it will be troublesome to you." "Indeed, uncle," answered Aladdin, "I cannot now; it is not troublesome to me: but I will as soon as I am up." The African magician was so obstinate, that he would have the lamp before he would help him up; and Aladdin, who had encumbered himself so much with his fruit that he could not well get at it, refused to give it to him till he was out of the cave. The African magician, provoked at this obstinate refusal, flew into a passion, threw a little of his incense into the fire, which he had taken care to keep in, and no sooner pronounced two magical words, than the stone which had closed the mouth of the cave moved into its place, with the earth over it in the same manner as it lay at the arrival of the magician and Aladdin.

8. **What did the magician put on one of Aladdin's fingers? Write your answer in the box below.**

> The magician put a ring on Aladdins fingers

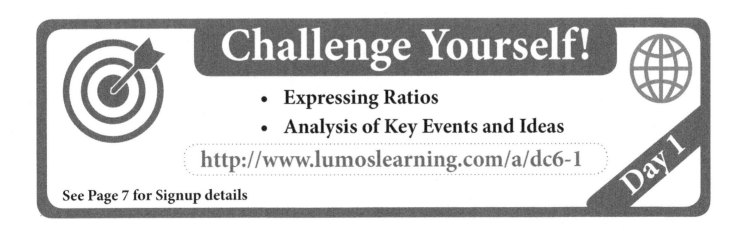

Unit Rates (6.RP.A.2)

Day 2

1. Which is a better price: 5 for $1.00, 4 for 85¢, 2 for 25¢, or 6 for $1.10?

   Ⓐ 5 for $1.00
   Ⓑ 4 for 85¢
   — Ⓒ 2 for 25¢
   Ⓓ 6 for $1.10

2. At grocery Store A, 5 cans of baked beans cost $3.45. At grocery Store B, 7 cans of baked beans cost $5.15. At grocery Store C, 4 cans of baked beans cost $2.46. At grocery Store D, 6 cans of baked beans cost $4.00. How much money would you save if you bought 20 cans of baked beans from grocery store C than if you bought 20 cans of baked beans from grocery store A?

   Ⓐ $1.75
   Ⓑ $1.25
   Ⓒ $1.50
   Ⓓ 95¢

3. Beverly drove from Atlantic City to Newark. She drove for 284 miles at a constant speed of 58 mph. How long did it take Beverly to complete the trip?

   Ⓐ 4 hours and 45 minutes
   Ⓑ 4 hours and 54 minutes
   Ⓒ 4 hours and 8 minutes
   Ⓓ 4 hours and 89 minutes

4. The bag of apples shown in the picture, costs $3.20. The cost of one apple is __40¢__.

40¢

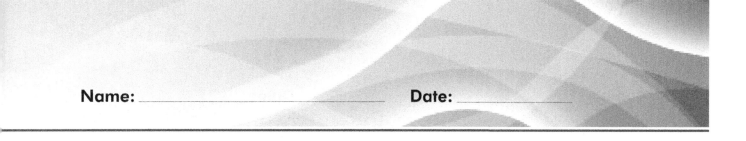

Conclusions Drawn from the Text (RL.6.1)

Day 2

Sarah's mother told her to carry an umbrella on that Thursday morning before she left home for school, but Sarah did not want to do that. She already had her backpack and a gift for her friend to take with her. She just did not think it was necessary.

5. **What can you infer about Sarah?**

    Ⓐ   She is stubborn and only wants to do things if they seem right to her.
    Ⓑ   She does not like her mother.
    Ⓒ   She doesn't like getting wet.
    Ⓓ   She is a very obedient child.

6. **What can you infer about the weather on that Thursday morning?**

    Ⓐ   It was raining
    Ⓑ   It was snowing
    Ⓒ   It was going to rain
    Ⓓ   It was a warm day

The boy returned home a little late from school. He threw his coat as he walked in. He walked past his parents without greeting them. He headed straight to his room, slamming the door after him. He threw himself face down on his bed and lay there.

7. **How is he feeling?**

    Ⓐ   very delighted
    Ⓑ   very disappointed
    Ⓒ   very scared
    Ⓓ   very excited

The leaves were changing colors and there were pumpkins in people's yards.

8. Which season is being described in this line?

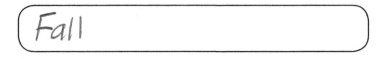

Fall

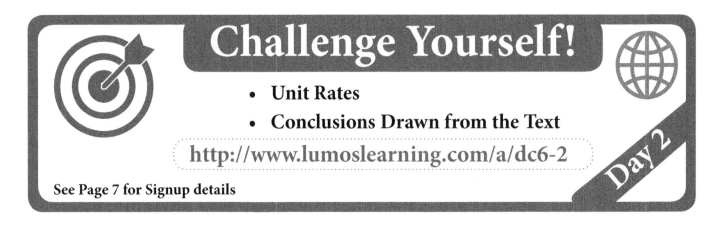

Challenge Yourself!

- Unit Rates
- Conclusions Drawn from the Text

http://www.lumoslearning.com/a/dc6-2

Day 2

See Page 7 for Signup details

Solving Real World Ratio Problems (6.RP.A.3)

Day 3

1. **How many kilograms are there in 375 grams?**

   Ⓐ 3,750 kg
   Ⓑ 37.5 kg
   Ⓒ 3.75 kg
   Ⓓ 0.375 kg

2. **How many inches are there in 2 yards?**

   Ⓐ 24 in
   Ⓑ 36 in
   Ⓒ 48 in
   Ⓓ 72 in

3. **What is 50% of 120?**

   Ⓐ 50
   Ⓑ 60
   Ⓒ 70
   Ⓓ 55

4. **Look at the ratio information found in the table below. Complete the table by correctly filling in the missing information.**

Feet	Yards
3	1
6	2½
9	3
15	5
24	8

Development of Ideas (RL.6.2)

Day 3

I always try to do what I have promised to do. If I say I will arrive at 5:15, I try to be there at 5:15. I don't lie or deliberately withhold information. I don't try to trick or confuse others. My friends trust me with their secrets, and I don't tell them to anyone else. I understand that you are looking for a trustworthy employee.

5. **Select the concluding sentence that most completely summarizes the argument in the passage.**

    Ⓐ   If you are looking for an employee who doesn't lie, then you should hire me.
    Ⓑ   If you are looking for an employee who needs to be at work at 5:15, then you should hire me.
    Ⓒ   If you are looking for a trustworthy person, you should hire me.
    Ⓓ   I believe I would make a very good employee and would love to be considered for a position at your company.

If I am chosen to be class president, I will represent you on the Student Council. I will listen to your requests and be sure that they are heard. I will show up for meetings. I will try to make our school a better place.

6. **Select the concluding sentence that most completely summarizes the argument in the passage.**

    Ⓐ   If you vote for me, I will be a good class president.
    Ⓑ   I am a good leader.
    Ⓒ   I will work towards scrapping exams.
    Ⓓ   The food in the cafeteria is awful.

Cats do not require as much attention as dogs. Dogs love you, and they want you to love them back. Cats are independent creatures. They don't need to be petted all the time. If you go on vacation for a few days, your dog may get lonely and refuse to eat, but your cat won't care.

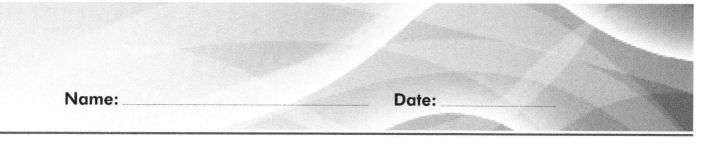

7. **Select the concluding sentence that most completely summarizes the argument in the passage.**

   Ⓐ If you really want a pet, it would be a good idea to get a cat and a dog.
   Ⓑ If you don't have a lot of time to care for a pet, a dog is a better choice for you than a cat.
   Ⓒ Vacations are a good idea if you have a cat as a pet.
   Ⓓ If you don't have a lot of time to care for a pet, a cat is a better choice for you than a dog.

Excerpt from Arabian Nights, Aladdin

Read the below passage and answer the questions.

After these words, the magician drew a ring off his finger, and put it on one of Aladdin's, telling him that it was a preservative against all evil, while he should observe what he had prescribed to him. After this instruction he said: "Go down boldly, child, and we shall both be rich all our lives."

Aladdin jumped into the cave, descended the steps, and found the three halls just as the African magician had described. He went through them with all the precaution the fear of death could inspire; crossed the garden without stopping, took down the lamp from the niche, threw out the wick and the liquor, and, as the magician had desired, put it in his vest band. But as he came down from the terrace, he stopped in the garden to observe the fruit, which he only had a glimpse of in crossing it. All the trees were loaded with extraordinary fruit, of different colors on each tree. Some bore fruit entirely white, and some clear and transparent as crystal; some pale red, and others deeper; some green, blue, and purple, and others yellow: in short, there were fruits of all colours. The white were pearls; the clear and transparent, diamonds; the deep red, rubies; the green, emeralds; the blue, turquoises; the purple, amethysts; and those that were of yellow cast, sapphires. Aladdin was altogether ignorant of their worth, and would have preferred figs and grapes, or any other fruits. But though he took them only for colored glass of little value, yet he was so pleased with the variety of the colors, and the beauty and extraordinary size of the seeming fruit, that he resolved to gather some of every sort; and accordingly filled the two new purses his uncle had bought for him with his clothes. Some he wrapped up in the skirts of his vest, which was of silk, large and full, and he crammed his bosom as full as it could hold.

Aladdin, having thus loaded himself with riches, returned through the three halls with the same precaution, made all the haste he could, that he might not make his uncle wait, and soon arrived at the mouth of the cave, where the African magician expected him with the utmost impatience. As soon as Aladdin saw him, he cried out: "Pray, uncle, lend me your hand, to help me out." "Give me the lamp first," replied the magician; "it will be troublesome to you." "Indeed, uncle," answered Aladdin, "I cannot now; it is not troublesome to me: but I will as soon as I am up." The African magician was so obstinate, that he would have the lamp before he would help him up; and Aladdin, who had encumbered himself so much with his fruit that he could not well get at it, refused to give it to him till he was out of the cave.

The African magician, provoked at this obstinate refusal, flew into a passion, threw a little of his incense into the fire, which he had taken care to keep in, and no sooner pronounced two magical words, than the stone which had closed the mouth of the cave moved into its place, with the earth over it in the same manner as it lay at the arrival of the magician and Aladdin.

8. The ring was a _____ against all evil. Write your answer in the box below.

> Preservative

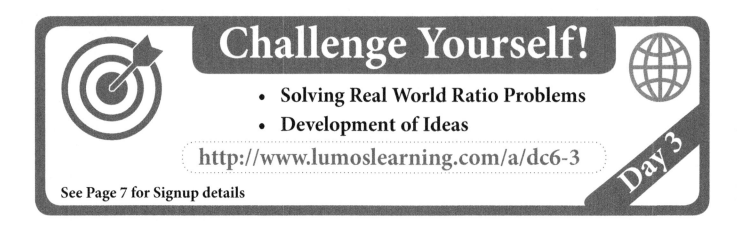

Solving Unit Rate Problems (6.RP.A.3.B)

Day 4

1. A 12 pack of juice pouches costs $6.00. How much does one juice pouch cost?

   Ⓐ $0.02
   Ⓑ $0.20
   Ⓒ $0.50
   Ⓓ $0.72

2. Eli can ride his scooter 128 miles on one tank of gas. If the scooter has a 4 gallon gas tank, how far can Eli ride on one gallon of gas?

   Ⓐ 64 miles per gallon
   Ⓑ 32 miles per gallon
   Ⓒ 512 miles per gallon
   Ⓓ 20 miles per gallon

3. Clifton ran 6 miles in 39 minutes. At this rate, how much time Clifton takes to run one mile?

   Ⓐ 13 minutes
   Ⓑ 12 minutes
   Ⓒ 7.2 minutes
   Ⓓ 6 minutes and 30 seconds

4. John paid $15 for 3 cheeseburgers. What is the rate of one cheeseburger? Enter your answer in the box below.

   $ 5

Day 4

One evening, long after most people had gone to bed, a friend and I were making our way merrily back home through the silent and almost deserted streets. We had been to a musical show and were talking about the actor we had seen and heard in it.

"That show made him a star overnight," said my friend about one of the actors. "He was completely unknown before and now thousands of teenagers send him chocolates and love letters through the mail."

"I thought he was quite good," I said, "but not worth thousands of love letters daily. As a matter of fact, one of his songs gave me a pain."

"What was that?" my friend asked. "Sing to me." I burst into a parody of the song.

"Be quiet for heaven's sake!" My friend gave me an astonished look. "You'll give everybody a fright and wake people up for miles around."

"Never mind," I said, intoxicated with the sound of my own voice. "I don't care. How does it matter?"

And I went on singing the latest tunes at the top of my voice.

Presently there came behind us the sound of heavy footsteps and before you could say "Jack Robinson" a policeman was standing in front of me, his notebook open, and a determined look on his face.

"Excuse me, sir," he said. "You have a remarkable voice, if I may say so. Who taught you to sing? I'd very much like to find someone who can give my daughter singing lessons. Would you be kind enough to tell me your name and address? Then my wife or I can drop you a line and discuss the matter."

5. **What probably happened at the end of the story?**

   Ⓐ Both the friends went home and had dinner
   Ⓑ The writer gave the policeman his name and address.
   Ⓒ The policeman arrested both the friends
   Ⓓ They went to see another musical show

Thomas is on the football team, the basketball team, and the hockey team. He even likes to run when he has free time.

6. By reading this you can conclude that _____?

Michael decided to climb a ladder to get his frisbee that landed on the roof. His father always told him to be careful when using a ladder because ladders were dangerous. Michael put on his bike helmet, asked his friend to hold the ladder, and put one hand in front of the other while climbing, never letting go of the ladder.

7. What can you conclude about climbing a ladder?

   Ⓐ   It is a lot of fun.
   Ⓑ   It is easy if you know what to do.
   Ⓒ   You should only climb a ladder if you are over 13 years old.
   Ⓓ   It can be very dangerous.

On the first day of school there are many supplies that a student needs. Every student needs a notebook, pencils, pens, highlighters, and the most important, a calendar.

8. What sentence below most closely agrees with these sentences?

   Ⓐ   All of these items help a student stay organized throughout the year.
   Ⓑ   These items are only helpful for students who enjoy math.
   Ⓒ   These items are expensive, so only buy a few of them.
   Ⓓ   You may not need all these items to stay organized.

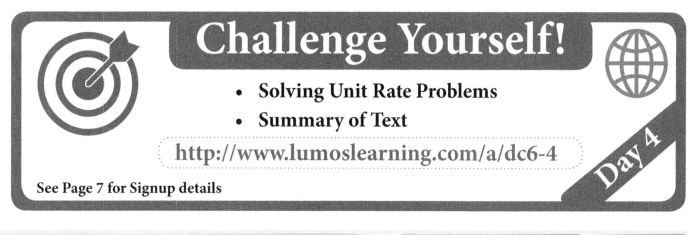

Challenge Yourself!

- **Solving Unit Rate Problems**
- **Summary of Text**

http://www.lumoslearning.com/a/dc6-4

Day 4

See Page 7 for Signup details

Finding Percent (6.RP.A.3.C)

Day 5

1. What is 25% of 24?

   Ⓐ 5
   Ⓑ 6
   Ⓒ 11
   Ⓓ 17

2. What is 15% of 60?

   Ⓐ 9
   Ⓑ 12
   Ⓒ 15
   Ⓓ 25

3. 9 is what percent of 72?

   Ⓐ 7.2%
   Ⓑ 8%
   Ⓒ 12.5%
   Ⓓ 14%

4. The following items were bought on sale. Complete the missing information.

Item Purchased	Original Price	Amount of Discount	Amount Paid
Video Game	$80	20%	$64
Movie Ticket	$14	20%	$11.20
Laptop	$1,000	25%	$750
Shoes	$55.00	10%	$49.5

Day 5

Characters Responses and Changes (RL.6.3)

One evening, long after most people had gone to bed, a friend and I were making our way merrily back home through the silent and almost deserted streets. We had been to a musical show and were talking about the actor we had seen and heard in it.

"That show made him a star overnight," said my friend about one of the actors. "He was completely unknown before and now thousands of teenagers send him chocolates and love letters through the mail."

"I thought he was quite good," I said, "but not worth thousands of love letters daily. As a matter of fact, one of his songs gave me a pain."

"Which was that?" my friend asked. "Sing to me." I burst into a parody of the song.

"Be quiet for heaven's sake!" My friend gave me an astonished look. "You'll give everybody a fright and wake people up for miles around."

"Never mind," I said, intoxicated with the sound of my own voice. "I don't care. Why does it matter?"

And I went on singing the latest tunes at the top of my voice. Presently there came behind us the sound of heavy footsteps and before you could say "Jack Robinson" a policeman was standing in front of me, his notebook open, and a determined look on his face.

"Excuse me, sir," he said. "You have a remarkable voice, if I may say so. Who taught you to sing? I'd very much like to find someone who can give my daughter singing lessons. Would you be kind enough to tell me your name and address? Then my wife or I can drop you a line and discuss the matter."

5. **Who are the three characters in the above passage?**

   Ⓐ the writer, the writer's friend, and the actor
   Ⓑ the writer, the writer's friend, and the singer
   Ⓒ the neighbors, the policeman, and his friend
   Ⓓ the writer, the writer's friend, and the policeman

6. Who were the writer and his friend referring to when they were talking and said "his songs"?

Ⓐ their neighbors
Ⓑ the policeman
Ⓒ the actor who sang in the musical show
Ⓓ the friend

Realizing his son's dog was still in the burning building, the dad ran back into the building.

7. A character trait of the father is _____.

Ⓐ Nervous
Ⓑ Scared
Ⓒ Carefree
Ⓓ Selfless

Excerpt from Arabian Nights, Aladdin

Read the below passage and answer the questions.

After these words, the magician drew a ring off his finger, and put it on one of Aladdin's, telling him that it was a preservative against all evil, while he should observe what he had prescribed to him. After this instruction he said: "Go down boldly, child, and we shall both be rich all our lives."
Aladdin jumped into the cave, descended the steps, and found the three halls just as the African magician had described. He went through them with all the precaution the fear of death could inspire; crossed the garden without stopping, took down the lamp from the niche, threw out the wick and the liquor, and, as the magician had desired, put it in his vestband. But as he came down from the terrace, he stopped in the garden to observe the fruit, which he only had a glimpse of in crossing it. All the trees were loaded with extraordinary fruit, of different colours on each tree. Some bore fruit entirely white, and some clear and transparent as crystal; some pale red, and others deeper; some green, blue, and purple, and others yellow: in short, there were fruits of all colours. The white were pearls; the clear and transparent, diamonds; the deep red, rubies; the green, emeralds; the blue, turquoises; the purple, amethysts; and those that were of yellow cast, sapphires. Aladdin was altogether ignorant of their worth, and would have preferred figs and grapes, or any other fruits. But though he took them only for coloured glass of little value, yet he was so pleased with the variety of the colours, and the beauty and extraordinary size of the seeming fruit, that he resolved to gather some of every sort; and accordingly filled the two new purses his uncle had bought for him with his clothes.

Some he wrapped up in the skirts of his vest, which was of silk, large and full, and he crammed his bosom as full as it could hold.

Aladdin, having thus loaded himself with riches, returned through the three halls with the same precaution, made all the haste he could, that he might not make his uncle wait, and soon arrived at the mouth of the cave, where the African magician expected him with the utmost impatience. As soon as Aladdin saw him, he cried out: "Pray, uncle, lend me your hand, to help me out." "Give me the lamp first," replied the magician; "it will be troublesome to you." "Indeed, uncle," answered Aladdin, "I cannot now; it is not troublesome to me: but I will as soon as I am up." The African magician was so obstinate, that he would have the lamp before he would help him up; and Aladdin, who had encumbered himself so much with his fruit that he could not well get at it, refused to give it to him till he was out of the cave. The African magician, provoked at this obstinate refusal, flew into a passion, threw a little of his incense into the fire, which he had taken care to keep in, and no sooner pronounced two magical words, than the stone which had closed the mouth of the cave moved into its place, with the earth over it in the same manner as it lay at the arrival of the magician and Aladdin.

8. **Why did the magician get angry with Aladdin on his return?**
   Write your answer in the box below.

The magician gave him the lamp

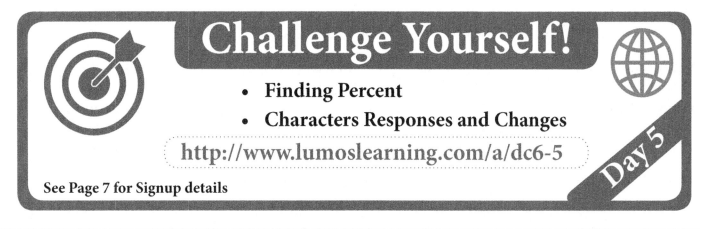

Challenge Yourself!

- **Finding Percent**
- **Characters Responses and Changes**

http://www.lumoslearning.com/a/dc6-5

Day 5

See Page 7 for Signup details

Learn Sign Language

What is American Sign Language?
American Sign Language (ASL) is a complete, complex language that employs signs made by moving the hands combined with facial expressions and postures of the body. It is the primary language of many North Americans who are deaf and is one of several communication options used by people who are deaf or hard-of-hearing.

Where did ASL originate?
The exact beginnings of ASL are not clear, but some suggest that it arose more than 200 years ago from the intermixing of local sign languages and French Sign Language (LSF, or Langue des Signes Française). Today's ASL includes some elements of LSF plus the original local sign languages, which over the years have melded and changed into a rich, complex, and mature language. Modern ASL and modern LSF are distinct languages and, while they still contain some similar signs, can no longer be understood by each other's users.

Source: https://www.nidcd.nih.gov/health/american-sign-language

Why should one learn sign language?

Enrich your cognitive skills: Sign language can enrich the cognitive development of a child. Since, different cognitive skills can be acquired as a child, learning sign language, can be implemented with practice and training in early childhood.

Make new friends: You could communicate better with the hearing-impaired people you meet, if you know the sign language, it is easier to understand and communicate effectively.

Volunteer: Use your ASL skills to interpret as a volunteer. volunteers can help in making a real difference in people's lives, with their time, effort and commitment.

Bilingual: If you are monolingual, here is an opportunity to become bilingual, with a cause.

Private chat: It would be useful to converse with a friend or in a group without anyone understanding, what you are up to.

Let's Learn the Alphabets

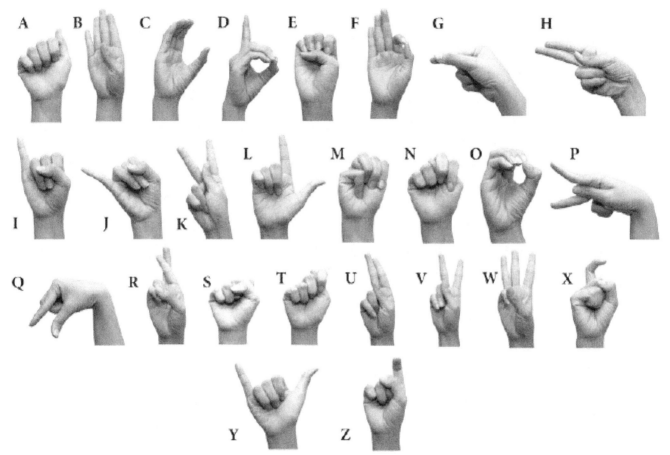

Sign language is fun if it is practiced with friends!
Partner with your friends or family members and try the following activities.

Activity

1. Communicate the following to your friend using the ASL.
   - **USA**
   - **ASL**

If your friend hasn't mastered the ASL yet, give the above alphabet chart to your friend.

2. Try saying your name in ASL using the hand gestures.

3. Have your friend communicate a funny word using ASL and you try to read it without the help of the chart. List the words you tried below.

Let's Learn Some Words

RED

ORANGE

YELLOW

GREEN

PURPLE

BLUE

EAT

DRINK

MORE

PLEASE

THANK YOU

SORRY

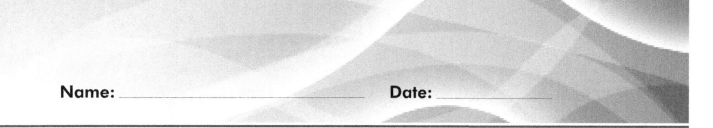

Let's Learn the Numbers

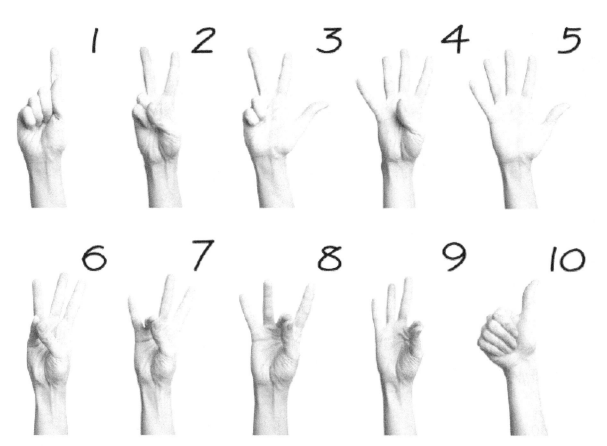

Activity:

1. Share your postal code through ASL to your friend.
2. Communicate your home phone number in ASL to your friend.

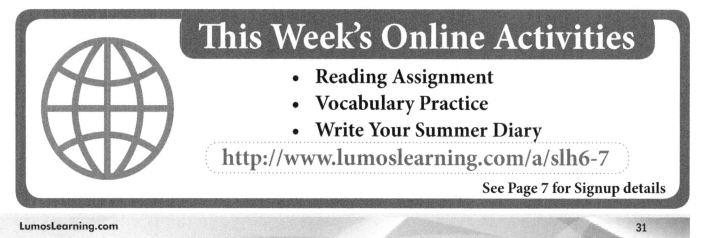

This Week's Online Activities

- Reading Assignment
- Vocabulary Practice
- Write Your Summer Diary

http://www.lumoslearning.com/a/slh6-7

See Page 7 for Signup details

Week 2 Summer Practice

Measurement Conversion (6.RP.A.3.D)

Day 1

1. Owen is 69 inches tall. How tall is Owen in feet?

   Ⓐ 5.2 feet
   Ⓑ 5.75 feet
   Ⓒ 5.9 feet
   Ⓓ 6 feet

2. What is 7 gallons 3 quarts expressed as quarts?

   Ⓐ 4.75 quarts
   Ⓑ 28 quarts
   Ⓒ 29.2 quarts
   Ⓓ 31 quarts

3. How many centimeters in 3.7 kilometers?

   Ⓐ 0.000037 cm
   Ⓑ 0.037 cm
   Ⓒ 3700 cm
   Ⓓ 370,000 cm

4. Use the chart provided to fill in the missing values in the table below.

1 L	1000 ml
1 g	1000 mg
1 m	1000 mm

3	L		ml
	g	5000	mg
	m	8000	mm
12	L		ml
20	g		mg

Figurative Words and Phrases (RL.6.4)

Day 1

5. Choose the sentence below that is closest in meaning to the figurative expression.

Edgar was dead to the world when we got home.

Ⓐ Edgar was asleep when we got home.
Ⓑ Edgar was not moving or breathing.
Ⓒ Edgar had a head injury and was unconscious.
Ⓓ Edgar was not at home.

6. Choose the sentence below that is closest in meaning to the figurative expression.

You'd better go home; you're in hot water.

Ⓐ You'd better go home; you're in trouble
Ⓑ You'd better go home; you'll find hot water there.
Ⓒ You'd better go home; you are sweating.
Ⓓ You'd better go home and drink hot water.

7. Choose the sentence below that is closest in meaning to the figurative expression.

He put all the papers in the circular file.

Ⓐ He put the papers in the wastebasket.
Ⓑ He rolled up all the papers.
Ⓒ He put the papers in the round file cabinet.
Ⓓ He put the papers on the circular table.

8. Choose the sentence below that is closest in meaning to the figurative expression.

Don't bug me!

Ⓐ   Don't bother me.
Ⓑ   Don't sneak.
Ⓒ   Don't tell me anything about yourself.
Ⓓ   Don't try to get the better of me.

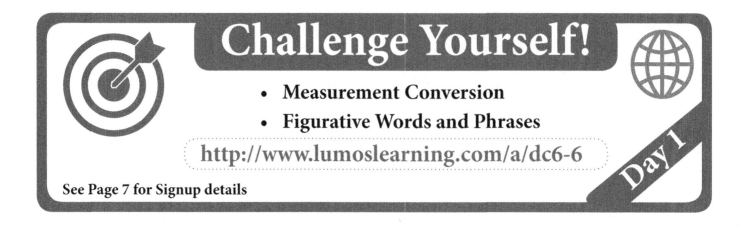

Challenge Yourself!

- **Measurement Conversion**
- **Figurative Words and Phrases**

http://www.lumoslearning.com/a/dc6-6

Day 1

See Page 7 for Signup details

Name: ______________________ Date: ______________

Division of Fractions (6.NS.A.1)

Day 2

1. **What is the quotient of 20 divided by one-fourth?**

   Ⓐ 80
   Ⓑ 24
   Ⓒ 5
   Ⓓ 15

2. **Calculate:** $1\frac{1}{2} \div \frac{3}{4} =$

   Ⓐ 4
   Ⓑ $\frac{1}{2}$
   Ⓒ $\frac{3}{4}$
   Ⓓ 2

3. **Calculate:** $3\frac{2}{3} \div 2\frac{1}{6} =$

   Ⓐ $\frac{8}{13}$
   Ⓑ $\frac{12}{13}$
   Ⓒ $1\frac{5}{13}$
   Ⓓ $1\frac{9}{13}$

4. **Fill in the blank.**

   $\frac{1}{2} \div 4 =$ ___?

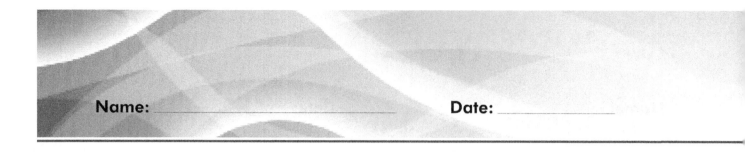

Connotative Words and Phrases (RL.6.4)

Day 2

5. Choose the best word to complete each sentence.

My friend is very careful about spending money. I admire that, so I call him _____.

   (A) Thrifty
   (B) Stingy
   (C) Miserly
   (D) Selfish

6. Choose the best word to complete each sentence.

My friend is very careful about spending money. I don't like that trait, so I call him _____.

   (A) Thrifty
   (B) Stingy
   (C) Rude
   (D) Mean

7. Choose the best word to complete each sentence.

I admire the man who jumped on the subway tracks to rescue a stranger. He was certainly _____.

   (A) Foolhardy
   (B) Undecided
   (C) Courageous
   (D) Stupid

8. What word describes this girl's behaviors?

The little girl threw her dolls all over her room, took her crayons and drew on the wall of her bedroom, and even pulled the dog's tail.

(A) snotty
(B) bratty
(C) nervous
(D) happy

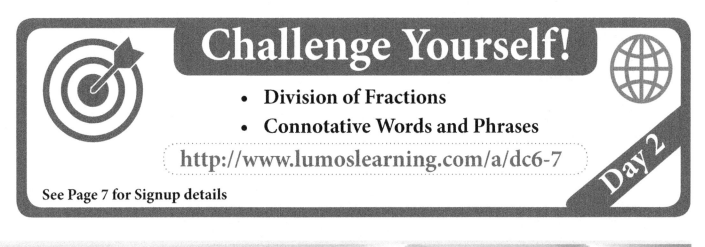

Challenge Yourself!

- **Division of Fractions**
- **Connotative Words and Phrases**

http://www.lumoslearning.com/a/dc6-7

See Page 7 for Signup details

Day 2

Division of whole Numbers (6.NS.B.2)

Day 3

1. A team of 12 players got an award of $1,800 for winning a championship football game. If the captain of the team is allowed to keep $315, how much money would each of the other players get? (Assume they split it equally.)

   Ⓐ $135
   Ⓑ $125
   Ⓒ $150
   Ⓓ $123.75

2. Peter gets a salary of $125 per week. He wants to buy a new television that costs $3,960. If he saves $55 per week, which of the following expressions could he use to figure out how many weeks it will take him to save up enough money to buy the new TV?

   Ⓐ $3,960 ÷ ($125 − $55)
   Ⓑ $3,960 − ($125)($55)
   Ⓒ ($3,960 ÷ $125) ÷ $55
   Ⓓ $3,960 ÷ $55

3. An expert typist typed 9,000 words in two hours. How many words per minute did she type?

   Ⓐ 4,500 words per minute
   Ⓑ 150 words per minute
   Ⓒ 75 words per minute
   Ⓓ 38 words per minute

4. Fill in the blank

   $40,950 ÷ \_\_\_\_ = 26$

Day 3

Meaning of Words and Phrases (RL.6.4)

"That show made him a star overnight", said my friend about one of the actors. "He was completely unknown before. And now thousands of teenagers send him chocolates and love letters in the mail."

5. **What does the above paragraph mean?**

    Ⓐ that the actor had poor acting skills
    Ⓑ that the actor had come to fame recently
    Ⓒ that nobody likes him now
    Ⓓ none of the above

The forest's sentinel
Glides silently across the hill
And perches in an old pine tree,
A friendly presence his!
No harm can come
From night bird on the prowl.
His cry is mellow,

Much softer than a peacock's call.
Why then this fear of owls
Calling in the night?
If men must speak,
Then owls must hoot-
They have the right.
On me it casts no spell:
Rather, it seems to cry,
"The night is good- all's well, all's well."

-- RUSKIN BOND

6. What is the poet talking about in the first stanza?

Ⓐ how the owl comes out into the night
Ⓑ how the owl catches its prey
Ⓒ how the owl is looking into the dark night
Ⓓ how the owl walks

7. What is the poet saying about the owl?

Ⓐ He is comparing the owl to a sentinel
Ⓑ He is describing the flight of the owl
Ⓒ He is saying that the owl is friendly and harmless
Ⓓ All of the above

Samantha was on the track team and was trying to perform her personal best in the high jump. She jumped 4 feet and made it over with ease. She then attempted her personal best at 5 feet, but did not make it on her first attempt. She tried four more times and, on the fifth try, she made it!

8. What is the meaning of this passage?

Ⓐ Keep trying to perform your personal best even if you fail the first time.
Ⓑ Only try something five times.
Ⓒ If you fail to perform your personal best, you may not succeed, even if you try again.
Ⓓ The faster you run, the higher you can go.

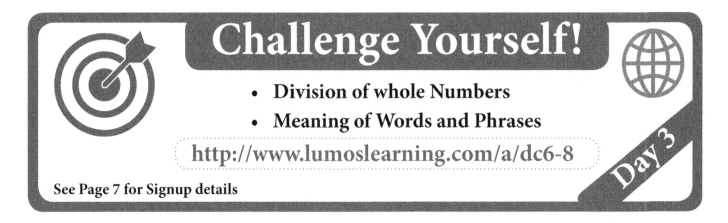

Challenge Yourself!

- **Division of whole Numbers**
- **Meaning of Words and Phrases**

http://www.lumoslearning.com/a/dc6-8

See Page 7 for Signup details

Day 3

Operations with Decimals (6.NS.B.3)

Day 4

1. Three friends went out to lunch together. Ben got a meal that cost $7.25, Frank got a meal that cost $8.16, and Herman got a meal that cost $5.44. If they split the check evenly, how much did they each pay for lunch? (Assume no tax)

    Ⓐ $6.95
    Ⓑ $7.75
    Ⓒ $7.15
    Ⓓ $6.55

2. Which of these is the standard form of twenty and sixty-three thousandths?

    Ⓐ 20.63000
    Ⓑ 20.0063
    Ⓒ 20.63
    Ⓓ 20.063

3. Mr. Zito bought a bicycle for $160. He spent $12.50 on repair charges. If he sold the same bicycle for $215, what would his profit be on the investment?

    Ⓐ $ 147.50
    Ⓑ $ 42.50
    Ⓒ $ 67.50
    Ⓓ $ 55.00

4. Fill in the blank.

    $7.1 \times 3.2 =$ ____

Day 4

The sky was dark and overcast. It had been raining all night long and there was no sign of it stopping. I thought that my Sunday would be ruined. As it poured outside, I settled down by the window to watch the rain. The park opposite my house looked even more green and fresh than usual. The branches of the tall trees swayed so hard in the strong wind that I thought they would break. A few children were splashing about in the mud puddles and having a wonderful time. I wished I could join them too! There were very few people out on the road and those who were hurried on their way, wrapped in raincoats and carrying umbrellas.

My mother announced that lunch was ready. It was piping hot and very welcoming in the damp weather. We spent the afternoon listening to music and to the downpour outside.

In the evening we chatted and made paper boats that we meant to sail in the stream of water outside. It was not a bad day after all!

5. **What is the setting of the above story?**

    Ⓐ The home of the writer
    Ⓑ The park
    Ⓒ The writer's village
    Ⓓ The writer's office

One evening, long after most people had gone to bed, a friend and I were making our way merrily back home through the silent and almost deserted streets. We had been to a musical show and were talking about the actor we had seen and heard in it.

"That show made him a star overnight," said my friend about one of the actors. "He was completely unknown before and now thousands of teenagers send him chocolates and love letters through the mail."

"I thought he was quite good," I said, "but not worth thousands of love letters daily. As a matter of fact, one of his songs gave me a pain."

"Which was that?" my friend asked. "Sing to me." I burst into a parody of the song.
"Be quiet for heaven's sake!" My friend gave me an astonished look. "You'll give everybody a fright and wake people up for miles around."

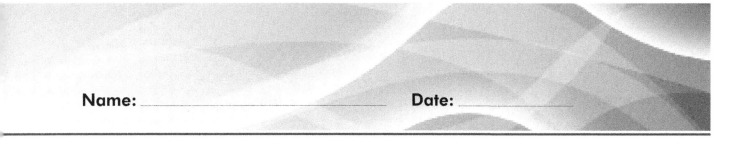

"Never mind," I said, intoxicated with the sound of my own voice. "I don't care. How does it matter?"

And I went on singing the latest tunes at the top of my voice. Presently there came behind us the sound of heavy footsteps and before you could say "Jack Robinson" a policeman was standing in front of me, his notebook open, and a determined look on his face.

"Excuse me, sir," he said. "You have a remarkable voice, if I may say so. Who taught you to sing? I'd very much like to find someone who can give my daughter singing lessons. Would you be kind enough to tell me your name and address? Then my wife or I can drop you a line and discuss the matter."

6. What detail in the above story tells us that it took place late in the night?

Ⓐ   We had been to a musical show
Ⓑ   "Be quiet for heaven's sake."
Ⓒ   One evening, long after most people had gone to bed
Ⓓ   And I went on singing the latest tunes at the top of my voice

The thieves intended to rob the bank around dinner time. They figured most people would be home eating with their families, so it would be easy for them to get in and out of the big green and gold bank.

7. What is the setting of the story?

Ⓐ   The bank on Green Street
Ⓑ   The bank on Green Street at 7 pm
Ⓒ   The green and gold bank at dinner time
Ⓓ   The green and gold bank in the morning

Tom looked out his window as he spoke on the phone with his mother. He told her about his day and the new job he just was offered. When Tom talked on the phone, he often looked out the window and would see Thomas Jefferson's monument. It was amazing that he lived in a city with so many beautiful, historical monuments, the White House and the U.S. Capitol.

8. Where does Tom live?

- Ⓐ New York City
- Ⓑ Washington State
- Ⓒ Delaware
- Ⓓ Washington, D.C.

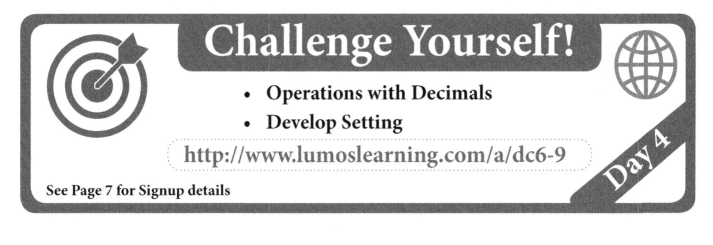

Challenge Yourself!

- **Operations with Decimals**
- **Develop Setting**

http://www.lumoslearning.com/a/dc6-9

See Page 7 for Signup details

Day 4

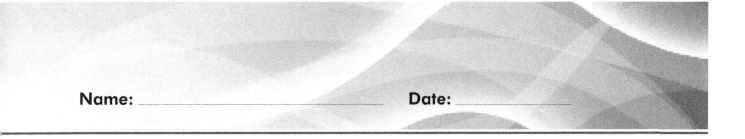

Day 5

1. **Which of these statements is true of the number 17?**

   Ⓐ It is a factor of 17.
   Ⓑ It is a multiple of 17.
   Ⓒ It is prime.
   Ⓓ All of the above are true.

2. **What are the single digit prime numbers**

   Ⓐ 2, 3, 5, and 7
   Ⓑ 1, 2, 3, 5, and 7
   Ⓒ 3, 5, and 7
   Ⓓ 1, 3, 5, and 7

3. **Which of the following sets below contains only prime numbers?**

   Ⓐ 7, 11, 49
   Ⓑ 7, 37, 51
   Ⓒ 7, 23, 47
   Ⓓ 2, 29, 93

4. **Fill in the blank.**

   The Greatest Common Factor (GCF) of 24, 36, and 48 is _____.

Author's Purpose in a Text (RL.6.6)

Day 5

In the original version of the story "The Three Little Pigs," the wolf chases the pigs and says he will huff and puff and blow their houses down.

The following paragraph is a different interpretation.

I've always been misunderstood. I'm allergic to hay. I can't help it that when I'm near hay, I huff and I puff and I sometimes blow things down. Also, I'm a vegetarian so I would never eat a pig! No one has any reason to be afraid of me, but sometimes they are. What happened to those poor little pigs is sad, but it was their own fault.

5. Who is talking in this passage? _____

6. How is the narrator's point of view different from the traditional one?

Ⓐ He claims that he had no intention of blowing down the pigs' houses or of eating them, but that his allergies were at fault.

Ⓑ He claims that he had no intention of blowing down the pigs' house, but wanted to eat them up.

Ⓒ He claims that he had no intention of blowing down the pigs' houses or of eating them, but he just wanted to scare them.

Ⓓ He claims that another wolf blew the pigs' houses down and blamed it on him.

7. Why does the narrator claim to have been misunderstood?

Ⓐ Because everyone has regarded him as a bully who wants to occupy weaker animals' houses
Ⓑ Because everyone has regarded him as a pig-killing villain when he had no such intention.
Ⓒ Because everyone has regarded him sick and allergy-ridden.
Ⓓ Because he is evil.

I was shaking like a leaf. My palms were sweaty and I was so nervous about my presentation.

8. What point of view is this from?

Ⓐ Third person omniscient
Ⓑ Second person
Ⓒ First person
Ⓓ Third person

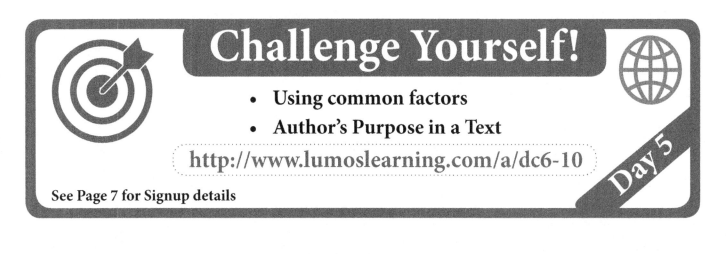

Challenge Yourself!

- Using common factors
- Author's Purpose in a Text

http://www.lumoslearning.com/a/dc6-10

Day 5

See Page 7 for Signup details

Gymnastics: Tips and Tricks for Skill Development

Gymnastics is a high energy sport that requires a combination of athleticism and artistry.

Because there are so many important parts of gymnastics, it can be hard to know what to focus on in order to improve. We have some great tips for budding gymnasts to improve their skills and ready themselves for new ones.

1. Practice Posture and Form.

Posture (also called form) is important in gymnastics: without proper form, you will not be able to carry out new skills.

Even if you are able to perform a skill with bad form, the execution will not be as attractive, and your scores will suffer in competition.

From the moment that you begin to learn a new skill, start by focusing on the beginning posture.

A lunge, for example, is a basic gymnastics skill. Once you have mastered a lunge, you move onto a handstand. Once you have mastered a handstand, you move on to front walkovers and front hand-springs.

However, if that original form is bad (your lunge), your handstands, front walkovers, and front hand-springs will not be as good as they could be.

Always pay very close attention and practice good form in everything you do. Practice form repetitively at home and in practice: practice makes perfect, especially with form.

2. Focus on Your Fingers and Toes!

Gymnastics requires that you think about so many body parts at once.

Because you must be paying attention to so many different parts of your body while performing a skill, you may forget about your fingers and toes.

Try to think of your fingers and toes like the exclamation points on a skill, and point them as you complete the skill.

Practice pointing your fingers and toes on each event so that it becomes second nature and you do it without thinking.

3. Strengthen Your Core.

Your "core" describes the muscles in your abdomen or stomach. These muscles play an important role in balance and form. If you have a weak core, you will struggle in many exercises and skills in gymnastics.

Without good core strength, your body will be "floppy" in motion, changing direction without you giving it permission to.

For this reason, your coach will likely lead you through strengthening or conditioning exercises meant to increase your core strength.

Exercises like crunches, v-ups, hanging leg raises, and hollow body rocking exercises are all good ways to increase the core strength that is so important in gymnastics.

Being consistent in strengthening exercises is also very important: your body grows stronger each time you perform the exercises, so it's important to keep doing them, so that they become easier with time.

4. Focus On Your Weak Spots.

Because gymnastics skills build on each other, it's important to pay close attention to your weak spots and events.

Even though most of us would rather perform skills we're good at, it's important to focus more of our attention on the skills that we're bad at in order to improve.

If there is a skill that needs more of your attention that can be safely practiced at home, do so!

However, always ask a parent or coach if a skill can be practiced safely at home, or if it should only be practiced with a coach at your gym.

5. Do Your Homework.

While many gymnastics skills cannot be performed safely at home, others can. Dance components of floor routines are especially easy to practice at home if you have enough space.

Dance is often overlooked in gymnastics, but it gives you a big competitive edge if you are able to perform those components of your floor and beam routines well.

Practicing the dance components of your routine at home also helps cement it into your mental and muscle memory.

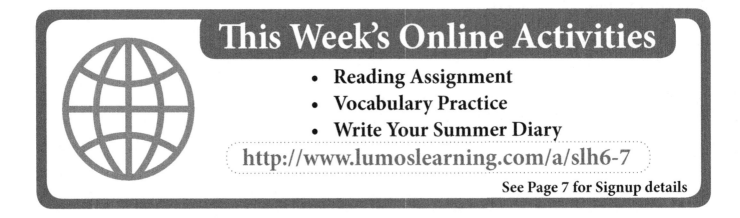

This Week's Online Activities

- **Reading Assignment**
- **Vocabulary Practice**
- **Write Your Summer Diary**

http://www.lumoslearning.com/a/slh6-7

See Page 7 for Signup details

Week 3 Summer Practice

Positive and Negative Numbers (6.NS.C.5)

Day 1

1. Larissa has $4\frac{1}{2}$ cups of flour. She is making cookies using a recipe that calls for $2\frac{3}{4}$ cups of flour. After baking the cookies how much flour will be left?

   Ⓐ $2\frac{3}{4}$ cups

   Ⓑ $2\frac{1}{4}$ cups

   Ⓒ $2\frac{3}{8}$ cups

   Ⓓ $1\frac{3}{4}$ cups

2. The accounting ledger for the high school band showed a balance of $2,123. They purchased new uniforms for a total of $2,400. How much must they deposit into their account in order to prevent it from being overdrawn?

   Ⓐ $382
   Ⓑ $462
   Ⓒ $4,000
   Ⓓ $277

3. Juan is climbing a ladder. He begins on the first rung, climbs up four rungs, but then slides down two rungs. What rung is Juan on?

   Ⓐ 2
   Ⓑ 3
   Ⓒ 4
   Ⓓ 5

4. **On a number line, how far apart are -27 and 30? Write your answer in the box below.**

Compare Authors Writing to Another (RL.6.9)

If your actions inspire others to dream more, learn more, do more and become more, you are a leader. - John Quincy Adams

The key to successful leadership today is influence, not authority.- Kenneth Blanchard

5. Pick the right statement that brings out the meaning of the above quotations.

Ⓐ Adams talks about actions, whereas Blanchard talks of authority.
Ⓑ Adams talks about leadership by inspiration, whereas Blanchard talks of leadership by influence.
Ⓒ Adams talks about inspiration, whereas Blanchard talks of influence.
Ⓓ Adams talks about leadership, whereas Blanchard talks of success.

Read the following passage and answer the question that follows.

The square is probably the best known of the quadrilaterals. It is defined as having all sides equal. All its interior angles are right angles (90°). From this it follows that the opposite sides are also parallel. A square is simply a specific case of a regular polygon, in this case with 4 sides. All the facts and properties described for regular polygons apply to a square.

The rectangle, like the square, is one of the most commonly known quadrilaterals. It is defined as having all four interior angles 90° (right angles). The opposite sides of a rectangle are parallel and congruent.

6. A similarity between a square and rectangle is that _____.

Ⓐ all the sides are equal in both the figures
Ⓑ only opposite sides are equal in both the figures
Ⓒ all the interior angles are right angles
Ⓓ none of the angles are right angles

7. Fill in the Blank

A difference between a square and rectangle is that _____.

When you wash dishes you want to make sure you use soap to scrub the dirt off and make sure you rinse them clean after.

8. Which of the tasks below are similar to washing dishes?

Ⓐ Cleaning your house
Ⓑ Washing the laundry
Ⓒ Folding your clothes
Ⓓ Cooking dinner

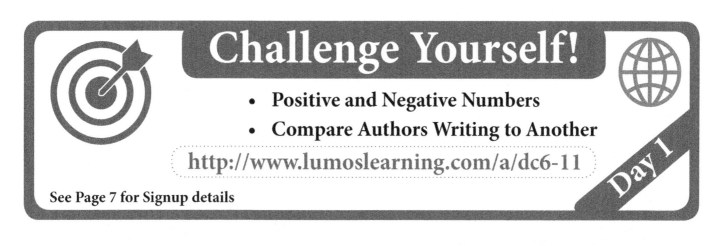

Challenge Yourself!

- **Positive and Negative Numbers**
- **Compare Authors Writing to Another**

http://www.lumoslearning.com/a/dc6-11

Day 1

See Page 7 for Signup details

Representing Negative Numbers (6.NS.C.6.A)

Day 2

1. Which of these numbers would be found closest to 0 on a number line?

   Ⓐ -5

   Ⓑ $-5\dfrac{1}{2}$

   Ⓒ $4\dfrac{1}{2}$

   Ⓓ -4

2. On a number line, how far apart are the numbers -5.5 and 7.5?

   Ⓐ 13 units
   Ⓑ 12 units
   Ⓒ 12.5 units
   Ⓓ 2 units

3. Which numbers does the following number line represent?

   ```
   ←——+——+——+——+——●——+——+——+——●——●——+——→
      -5  -4  -3  -2  -1  0   1   2   3   4   5
   ```

   Ⓐ $\{-2, 0, 5\}$
   Ⓑ $\{-3, -1, 4\}$
   Ⓒ $\{-1, 3, 5\}$
   Ⓓ $\{-1, 3, 4\}$

4. Which number(s) have a value lower than 3? Select all that apply.

   Ⓐ - 5
   Ⓑ 6
   Ⓒ -18
   Ⓓ -23
   Ⓔ 4

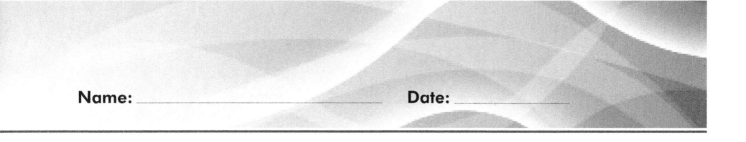
Cite Textual Evidence to Support Analysis (RI.6.1)

Day 2

Everywhere around us, there are millions of tiny living things called germs. They are so tiny that they can be seen only under the most powerful microscope. Some of these germs are no wider than twenty-five thousandths of an inch!

Louis Pasteur, the great French scientist, was the first to prove that germs exist. The germs in the air can be counted. The number of germs around us, especially in crowded rooms, is tremendous. Certain scientists counted 42,000 germs in approximately one cubic meter of air in a picture gallery when it was empty. But when the gallery was crowded with people, they found nearly 5,000,000 germs in the same place. In the open air germs are less abundant. There are fewer germs in country air than in town air. We see at once how important it is, therefore, to live as much as possible in the open air, and for the rooms we live in to always be well ventilated by fresh air.

5. According the passage, where will you find more germs?

- Ⓐ   In crowded spaces
- Ⓑ   In the country
- Ⓒ   In hospitals
- Ⓓ   In empty rooms

6. Which of the following statements can be concluded after reading the passage?

- Ⓐ   Louis Pasteur liked counting germs.
- Ⓑ   Germs are too small to be seen.
- Ⓒ   People have germs.
- Ⓓ   Fresher air has fewer germs.

Michael Jordan was the greatest basketball player of all time. When he played for the Chicago Bulls, they had one winning season after another. He scored more than 100 points in 1,108 games, won two Olympic gold medals, and was ranked #1 by ESPN Magazine. Chosen for the NBA All-Stars 14 times, Jordan was ten times the scoring champ, five times the Most Valuable Player, and six times the scoring champ of the NBA. When he began losing his hair, he shaved his head completely and started a fashion trend for other players. He was chosen to make an animated movie called "Space Jam" with Bugs Bunny. No other player has come close to those achievements.

7. Why did the author write this passage about Michael Jordan?

Ⓐ To tell about how Michael Jordan made a movie with Bugs Bunny.
Ⓑ To show what a great basketball player Michael Jordan is.
Ⓒ To give reader's Michael Jordan's life story.
Ⓓ To tell people what it is like to be a famous basketball player.

How does the body know to breathe and move?
The central nervous system tells the body what to do.
The nervous system is made up of nerves, the spinal cord and the brain.

8. From the above lines, we can infer that the nervous system is the _____ of the human body.
Fill in the blank by choosing the correct option from among the 4 options given below.

Ⓐ digesting system
Ⓑ breathing system
Ⓒ circulatory system
Ⓓ control system

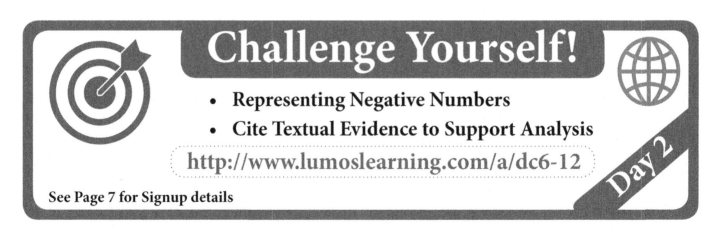

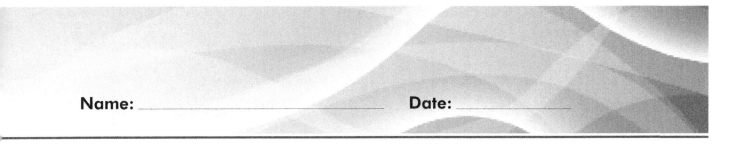

Day 3

1. In what Quadrant (I, II, III, IV) does the point (−12, 20) lie?

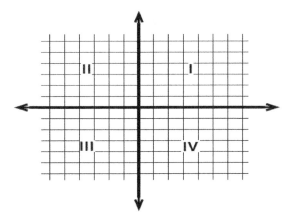

    Ⓐ Quadrant I
    Ⓑ Quadrant II
    Ⓒ Quadrant III
    Ⓓ Quadrant IV

2. In what Quadrant (I, II, III, IV) does the point (8, −9) lie?

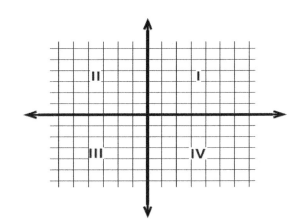

    Ⓐ Quadrant I
    Ⓑ Quadrant II
    Ⓒ Quadrant III
    Ⓓ Quadrant IV

3. In what Quadrant (I, II, III, IV) does the point (−0.75, −0.25) lie?

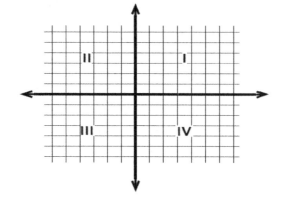

Ⓐ Quadrant I
Ⓑ Quadrant II
Ⓒ Quadrant III
Ⓓ Quadrant IV

4. What are the coordinates of point 'A' ? Enter your answer in the box below.

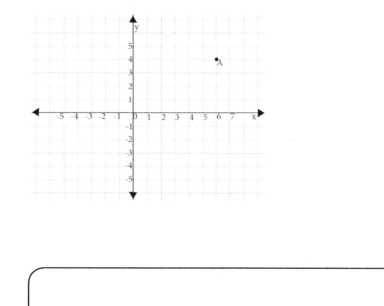

Day 3

1. Books were hard to get for the mountain men among the western settlers.
2. Sometimes a mountain man would carry a single battered book with him for years.
3. Some of the men had Bibles, and even more had Shakespeare's plays.
4. Shakespeare was a favorite with mountain men, even if they could not read.
5. When they found someone who could read, he was often asked to read one of Shakespeare's plays to a group over a campfire.
6. There were mountain men who could not sign their own names, but could quote passages of Shakespeare by heart.

5. Which sentence best shows the main idea of this paragraph?

Ⓐ Sentence #1
Ⓑ Sentence #6
Ⓒ Sentence #3
Ⓓ Sentence #5

6. Which two sentences best support the main idea- that mountain men liked Shakespeare, even if they could not read?

Ⓐ Sentences #2 and #6
Ⓑ Sentences #3 and #5
Ⓒ Sentences #1 and #2
Ⓓ Sentences #3 and #6

7. Which sentence does not directly support the main idea?

Ⓐ Sentence #2
Ⓑ Sentence #3
Ⓒ Sentence #5
Ⓓ Sentence #6

Washing clothes is a difficult task. The skill has to be learned and mastered. It is a tedious and tiresome process, which often discourages a person from going through the exercise. In spite of the availability of modern detergent powders, it remains a difficult task. An expert knows which parts of the dress need special care and attention. The collars of shirts and the seat and pockets of pants are generally dirtier than the other parts. But to wash well, what you require most is patience and the knowledge of the texture and quality of the cloth you are washing so that you can differentiate between clothes which can be put in warm water and which must never be washed in hot water. Woolens, silken and cotton clothes need different types of washing and detergents. One must have proper knowledge of these before washing clothes.

8. What is the above passage about?

Challenge Yourself!

- **Ordered Pairs**
- **Central Idea of Text**

http://www.lumoslearning.com/a/dc6-13

Day 3

See Page 7 for Signup details

Number Line & Coordinate Plane (6.NS.C.6.C)

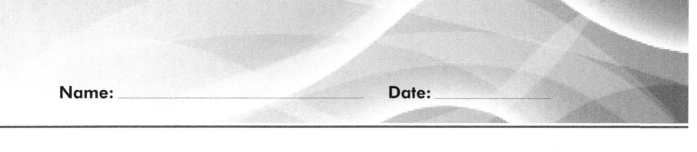

Day 4

1. What number does the dot represent on the number line?

    Ⓐ 12
    Ⓑ 13
    Ⓒ 14
    Ⓓ 15

2. What number does the dot represent on the number line?

    Ⓐ −2
    Ⓑ −1
    Ⓒ 0
    Ⓓ 1

3. What number does the dot represent on the number line?

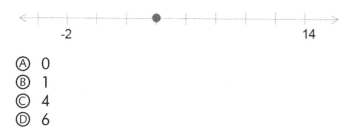

    Ⓐ 0
    Ⓑ 1
    Ⓒ 4
    Ⓓ 6

4. Choose the set of numbers that are correctly ordered from least to greatest. Use the number line to help you. Choose all answers that apply.

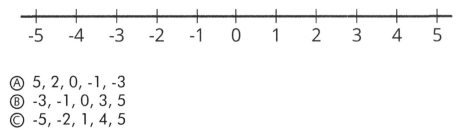

Ⓐ 5, 2, 0, -1, -3
Ⓑ -3, -1, 0, 3, 5
Ⓒ -5, -2, 1, 4, 5
Ⓓ 0, 1, 3, -4, -5
Ⓔ None of the above

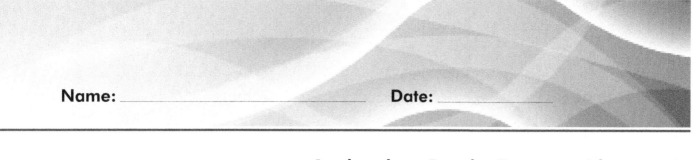

Analyze how People, Events, or Ideas are Presented in Text (RI.6.3)

Day 4

Everywhere around us, there are millions of tiny living things called germs. They are so tiny that they can be seen only under the most powerful microscope. Some of these germs are no wider than twenty-five thousandths of an inch!

Louis Pasteur, the great French scientist, was the first to prove that germs exist. The germs in the air can be counted. The number of germs around us, especially in crowded rooms, is tremendous. Certain scientists counted 42,000 germs in approximately one cubic meter of air in a picture gallery when it was empty. But when the gallery was crowded with people, they found nearly 5,000,000 germs in the same place. In the open air germs are less abundant. There are fewer germs in country air than in town air. We see at once how important it is, therefore, to live as much as possible in the open air, and for the rooms we live in to always be well ventilated by fresh air.

5. What is the main idea of the above passage?

Ⓐ Louis Pasteur was a great French scientist.
Ⓑ Germs are everywhere.
Ⓒ Germs are small.
Ⓓ Germs can be counted.

6. Which of the following details does NOT support the main idea of the passage?

Ⓐ Germs are tiny and can only be seen using powerful microscopes.
Ⓑ There are fewer germs in open air.
Ⓒ The more people you are around, the sicker you will become.
Ⓓ Germs are living things.

Books were hard to get for the mountain men among the western settlers. Sometimes a mountain man would carry a single battered book with him for years. Some of the men had Bibles, and even more had Shakespeare's plays. Shakespeare was a favorite with mountain men, even if they could not read. When they found someone who could read, he was often asked to read one of Shakespeare's plays to a group over a campfire. There were mountain men who could not sign their own names, but could quote passages of Shakespeare by heart.

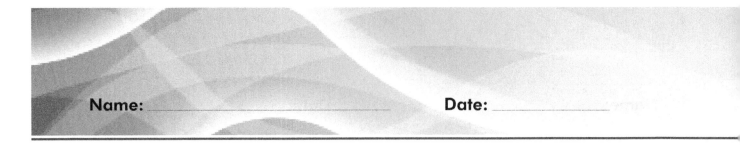
7. How does the author of the above passage show that books were important to mountain men?

    Ⓐ Books were hard for mountain men to get.
    Ⓑ Some mountain men had Shakespeare's plays.
    Ⓒ Some mountain men could quote Shakespeare.
    Ⓓ Not all mountain men could read.

Washing clothes is a difficult task. The skill has to be learned and mastered. It is a tedious and tiresome process, which often discourages a person from going through the exercise. In spite of the availability of modern detergent powders, it remains a difficult task. An expert knows which parts of the dress need special care and attention. The collars of shirts and the seat and pockets of pants are generally dirtier than the other parts. But to wash well, what you require most is patience and the knowledge of the texture and quality of the cloth you are washing so that you can differentiate between clothes which can be put in warm water and clothes which must never be washed in hot water. Woolens, silk and cotton clothes need different types of washing and detergents. One must have proper knowledge of these before washing clothes.

8. How does the author of the above passage illustrate that washing clothes is a difficult task? Circle the correct answer choice.

    Ⓐ By discussing the different types of washing machines.
    Ⓑ By pointing out that certain parts of clothing need special care and attention.
    Ⓒ By talking about all the different laundry detergent options.
    Ⓓ By explaining how time consuming laundry can be.

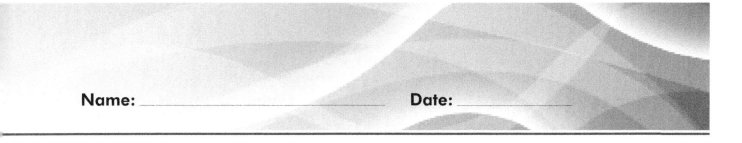
Day 5

1. Evaluate the following: $17 - |(7)(-3)|$

    (A) 38
    (B) −4
    (C) 4
    (D) 13

2. Evaluate the following: $16 + |(7)(-3) - 44| - 5$

    (A) 76
    (B) 86
    (C) 34
    (D) 44

3. Evaluate the following: $|15 - 47| + 9 - |(-2)(-4) - 17|$

    (A) 32
    (B) −32
    (C) 50
    (D) 76

4. What is the value of $|14| - |-28|$? Write your answer in the box below.

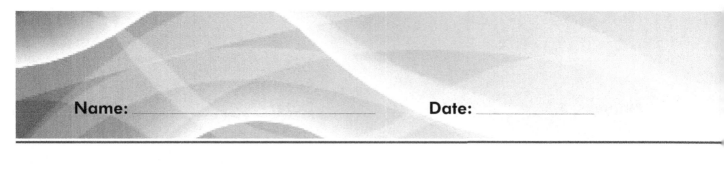

Determine Technical Meanings (RI.6.4)

Day 5

5. What is a synonym of a word?

ⓐ A word that has the same meaning as the given word.
ⓑ A word that has the opposite meaning of a given word.
ⓒ A word that has the same spelling as the given word.
ⓓ A word that has the same pronunciation as the given word.

6. Which of the following statements is true about antonyms?

ⓐ They have the same meaning as the given word.
ⓑ They are the definitions of a given word.
ⓒ They have the same sounds as a given word.
ⓓ They are the opposites of a given word.

The words "minute" (time) and "minute" (extremely small) are pronounced differently and have different meanings.

7. These types of words are called _____.

ⓐ Homophones
ⓑ Homonyms
ⓒ Homographs
ⓓ Homo-words

8. Which of the choices below is an example of an antonym?

Ⓐ Clever, crazy
Ⓑ Pretty, beautiful
Ⓒ Narrow, skinny
Ⓓ Abundant, scarce

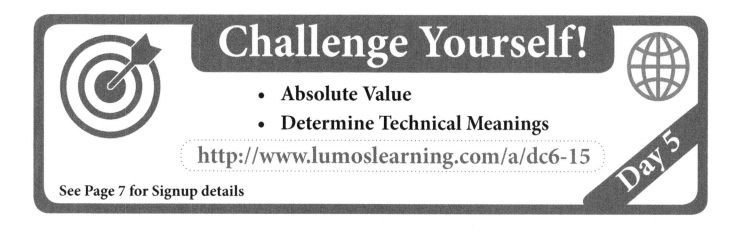

Challenge Yourself!

- **Absolute Value**
- **Determine Technical Meanings**

http://www.lumoslearning.com/a/dc6-15

Day 5

See Page 7 for Signup details

Draw and Color

Name: _____ Date: _____

Use the below space for your drawing activity.

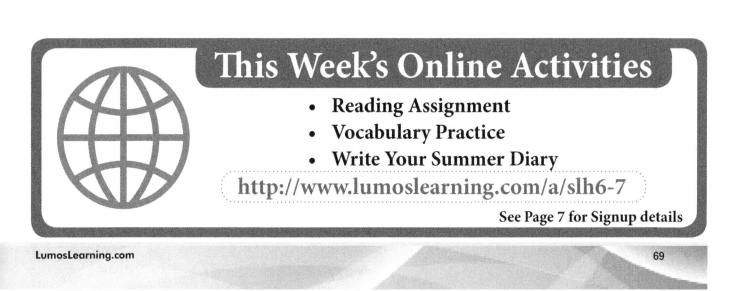

This Week's Online Activities

- Reading Assignment
- Vocabulary Practice
- Write Your Summer Diary

http://www.lumoslearning.com/a/slh6-7

See Page 7 for Signup details

Week 4 Summer Practice

Day 1

Rational Numbers in Context (6.NS.C.7.B)

1. Xavier has a golf score of −7 (We write −7 because it is 7 points below par) and Curtis has a golf score of −12. Who has the higher score?

   Ⓐ Xavier has the higher score.
   Ⓑ Curtis has the higher score.
   Ⓒ Because both scores are below par, neither one has the higher score.
   Ⓓ We cannot tell who has the higher score because we do not know what par is.

2. Kelly has read $\frac{5}{6}$ of a book. Helen has read $\frac{9}{12}$ of the same book. Who has read more of the book?

   Ⓐ $\frac{5}{6}$ is more than $\frac{9}{12}$ so Kelly has read more.

   Ⓑ $\frac{5}{6}$ is less than $\frac{9}{12}$ so Helen has read more.

   Ⓒ $\frac{5}{6}$ is the same as $\frac{9}{12}$ so both Kelly and Helen have read the same amount.

   Ⓓ We cannot tell who has read more because the fractions have different denominators.

3. The record low temperature for NY is −52°F. The record low temperature for Alaska is −80°F. Which of the following inequalities accurately compares these two temperatures?

   Ⓐ −52° < −80° F
   Ⓑ −80° > −52° F
   Ⓒ −52° = −80° F
   Ⓓ −52° > −80° F

4. Which temperature is hotter, 32 degrees or 56 degrees? Enter your answer in the box below.

Structure of Text (RI.6.5)

Day 1

5. **Identify where the underlined sentence below belongs in the paragraph.**

<u>**Start with the freshest bread you can find.**</u>

I will tell you how to make a perfect peanut butter sandwich.
Take the two pieces of bread.
Add a good-sized scoop of crunchy peanut butter, and be sure to spread it on both pieces of bread.
Find a jar of your favorite jam.
Use slightly less jam than peanut butter, and spread it on only one slice of bread.
Put the two slices together and cut the sandwich in half. Enjoy.

Ⓐ The missing sentence should be first.
Ⓑ The missing sentence should be second.
Ⓒ The missing sentence should be third.
Ⓓ The missing sentence should be fourth.

6. **Identify where the underlined sentence below belongs in the paragraph.**

<u>**During the pre-competition phase, continue the aerobic training, but add strength training and sprints.**</u>

Training for tennis can be broken down into four phases.
During the preparation phase, work on aerobic fitness with jogging, swimming, or cycling as you train heavily on the specifics of tennis.
While competing, training can ease up except for the specifics of tennis.
For several weeks after competition, rest from playing tennis but keep up your fitness by playing other sports.

Ⓐ The missing sentence should be first.
Ⓑ The missing sentence should be second.
Ⓒ The missing sentence should be third.
Ⓓ The missing sentence should be fourth.

7. The salutation in a business letter is what part of a letter?

Ⓐ Heading
Ⓑ Closing
Ⓒ Address and date
Ⓓ Greeting

8. Which of the following types of writing will most likely contain the most descriptive writing (imagery)? Circle the correct answer choice.

Ⓐ Letter of complaint to a store about a product that was faulty
Ⓑ Personal narrative about a rodeo
Ⓒ Descriptive paper about a winter day
Ⓓ Informative/Expository paper about snow

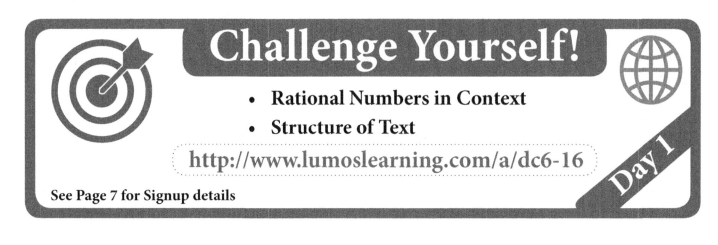

Challenge Yourself!

- **Rational Numbers in Context**
- **Structure of Text**

http://www.lumoslearning.com/a/dc6-16

See Page 7 for Signup details

Day 1

Interpreting Absolute Value (6.NS.C.7.C)

Day 2

1. What is the absolute value of the number represented by the Black dot plotted below?

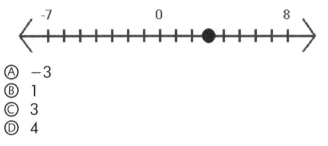

    Ⓐ −3
    Ⓑ 1
    Ⓒ 3
    Ⓓ 4

2. What is the absolute value of the number represented by the Black dot plotted below?

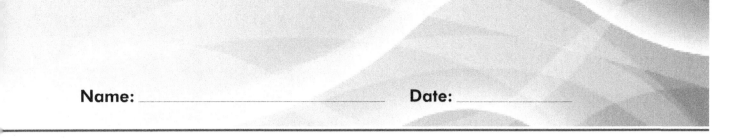

    Ⓐ −2
    Ⓑ −1
    Ⓒ 1
    Ⓓ 2

3. Which symbol will make the following a true statement? $|-27|$ _____ 19

    Ⓐ >
    Ⓑ <
    Ⓒ =
    Ⓓ ≤

4. Sequence the numbers as they would fall on the number line in order from least to greatest. Enter the correct answers in the boxes given below.

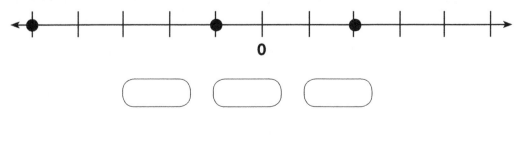

Determine Author's Point of View (RI.6.6)

Day 2

Dogs are better pets than cats for many reasons. Dogs are a man's best friend and can learn tricks. Dogs will get you things when you ask them to. Dogs will go walking or running with you to help keep you in shape. Dogs like to cuddle and protect their owners.

5. What is the purpose of the above passage?

Ⓐ   To inform
Ⓑ   To explain
Ⓒ   To persuade
Ⓓ   To entertain

If you invent a new word and enough people like it, you may find it in the dictionary. Dictionaries add new words as they come into common use. The fancy word for a brand-new word is "neologism." In 2011, the Merriam-Webster Collegiate Dictionary added some neologisms you probably know, such as "tweet," "fist bump," and "social media."

Some of the new words may not be so familiar.

- "Planking" is a game of lying face down, hands at your sides, in the most unusual place you can think of, and having your picture taken and posted on the internet.
- A "bromance" is a close friendship – but not a romance – between two men.
- A "robocall" is a call made automatically by a machine repeating a taped message.
- A "helicopter parent" is one who hovers over their children, becoming much too involved in their lives.
- And "crowdsourcing"? That's the way many people can each do a little bit of a very large project. The country of Iceland, for example, is crowdsourcing a new constitution for their country, so if you have an idea about what they ought to include, you can go online and send them your suggestion.

At the same time new words are being added, old words that are no longer widely recognized are dropped from the dictionary. This year, the dictionary deleted the words "growlery" (a room where you can go to complain) and "brabble" (another word for squabble). If you haven't heard those words before, you probably won't miss them!

6. What is the purpose of the passage above?

- Ⓐ To inform
- Ⓑ To explain
- Ⓒ To persuade
- Ⓓ To entertain

Eating carrots, broccoli and string beans are good for you. Making sure to have healthy vegetables in your diet is important. Some people think eating vegetables at one meal is good enough, but it isn't; you should eat vegetables at least 3 meals a day.

7. What is the purpose of the passage above?

- Ⓐ To convince the reader to eat more vegetables.
- Ⓑ To give information about different types of vegetables.
- Ⓒ To tell about a cartoon where the characters are played by vegetables.
- Ⓓ The help the reader understand there is nothing important about vegetables.

Michael Jordan was the greatest basketball player of all time. When he played for the Chicago Bulls, they had one winning season after another. He scored more than 100 points in 1,108 games, won two Olympic gold medals, and was ranked #1 by ESPN Magazine. Chosen for the NBA All-Stars 14 times, Jordan was ten times the scoring champ, five times the Most Valuable Player, and six times the scoring champ of the NBA. When he began losing his hair, he shaved his head completely and started a fashion trend for other players. He was chosen to make an animated movie called "Space Jam" with Bugs Bunny. No other player has come close to those achievements.

8. Why did the author write this passage about Michael Jordan?

Ⓐ   To tell about how Michael Jordan made a movie with Bugs Bunny.
Ⓑ   To show what a great basketball player Michael Jordan is.
Ⓒ   To give reader's Michael Jordan's life story.
Ⓓ   To tell people what it is like to be a famous basketball player.

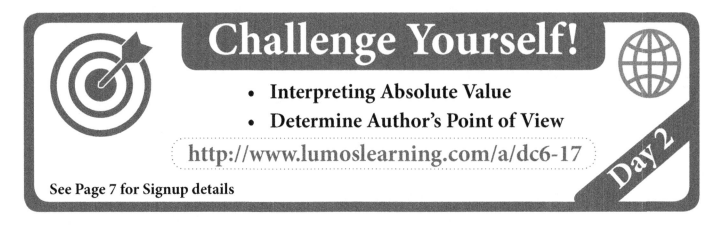

Challenge Yourself!

- **Interpreting Absolute Value**
- **Determine Author's Point of View**

http://www.lumoslearning.com/a/dc6-17

Day 2

See Page 7 for Signup details

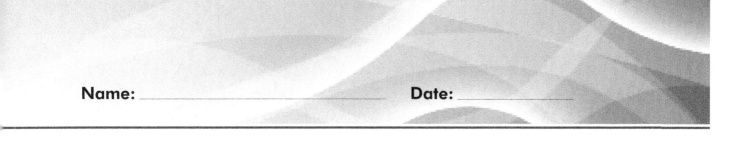
Comparisons of Absolute Value (6.NS.C.7.D)

Day 3

1. Which account balance represents the greater debt?
    $20, −$45, −$5, $10

    Ⓐ $20
    Ⓑ −$45
    Ⓒ −$5
    Ⓓ $10

2. Which of the following is the warmest temperature?
    5°F above zero, 6°F below zero, 10°F below zero, 2°F above zero

    Ⓐ 5°F above zero
    Ⓑ 6°F below zero
    Ⓒ 10°F below zero
    Ⓓ 2°F above zero

3. Anneliese spent $58.00 on music items and paid $35.00 on a lay-away item. If she has −142.00 left in her account, how much did she start with?

    Ⓐ $−49.00
    Ⓑ $93.00
    Ⓒ $135.00
    Ⓓ −$235.00

4. Find the Value of $|12| - |-11| =$ _____?

Evaluating Arguments in Text (RI.6.8)

Day 3

Michael Jordan was the greatest basketball player of all time. He scored more than 100 points in 1,108 games, won two Olympic gold medals, and was ranked #1 by ESPN Magazine. Chosen for the NBA All-Stars 14 times, Jordan was ten times the scoring champ, five times the Most Valuable Player, and six times the scoring champ of the NBA. No other player has come close to those achievements.

5. Identify the main idea – the claim – in the above persuasive paragraph. _____.

- (A) Jordan was six times the 'scoring champ' for NBA.
- (B) Jordan was chosen for the NBA All-Stars 14 times.
- (C) The claim is that Jordan was the greatest basketball player.
- (D) Jordan was a basketball player.

Michael Jordan was the greatest basketball player of all time. When he played for the Chicago Bulls, they had one winning season after another. When he began losing his hair, he shaved his head completely and started a fashion trend for other players. He was chosen to make an animated movie called "Space Jam" with Bugs Bunny. There are many good players, but Michael Jordan will always be my favorite.

6. The claim: Jordan was the greatest basketball player.

Details to support this claim include:_____.

- (A) He was the best player on the team.
- (B) When he began losing his hair, he shaved his head completely and started a fashion trend for other players.
- (C) He was chosen to make an animated movie called "Space Jam" with Bugs Bunny.
- (D) When he played for the Chicago Bulls, they had one winning season after another.

Running a marathon is a great accomplishment. Training for a marathon takes months. First, you have to start running short distances, and increase each week the distance you run. During your training, you will eventually start running 20 miles at a time. A full marathon is 26.2 miles and very hard for people to finish. With a little time, training, and hard work, anyone can run a marathon. Completing the marathon is a great accomplishment because it shows excellent dedication and athletic ability.

7. Identify the claim in this passage.

Ⓐ   Running a marathon requires you to train a lot.
Ⓑ   Running a marathon is a great accomplishment.
Ⓒ   Running requires excellent dedication.
Ⓓ   Not many people are able to complete a marathon.

Smartphones are the newest innovative technology out there. On the Smartphone you can video chat with your friends or family members to keep in touch. Smartphones also are a great way to stay organized and keep your life on track. Smartphones are an easy way to search the internet when you are out and need to find something quickly. They allow you to access tons of information.

8. Identify the claim in this passage.

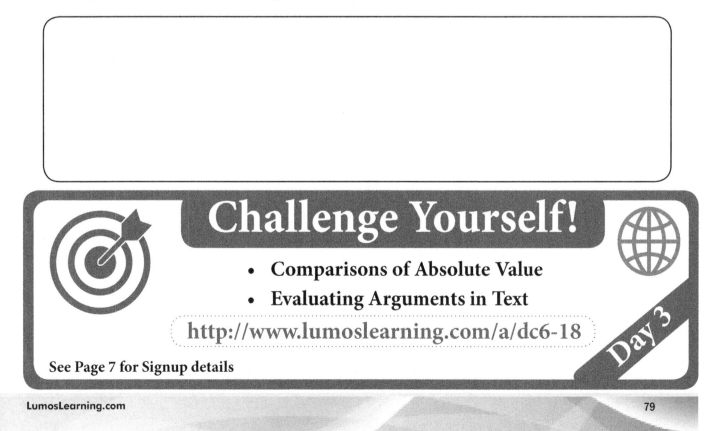

Challenge Yourself!

- **Comparisons of Absolute Value**
- **Evaluating Arguments in Text**

http://www.lumoslearning.com/a/dc6-18

Day 3

See Page 7 for Signup details

Coordinate Plane (6.NS.C.8)

Day 4

1. Ricky and Becca are going hiking. Below is the map that they are using. They start out at $(-3.6, -2.6)$. They hike four units to the east and six units to the north. What are the coordinates of their new location? (Note: North is up on this map.)

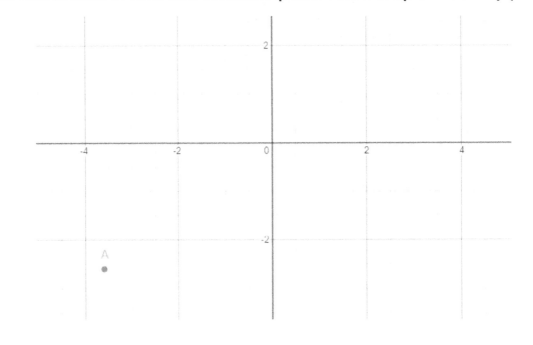

Ⓐ (0.6, 3.6)
Ⓑ (0.4, 3.4)
Ⓒ (0.4, 3.6)
Ⓓ (1.6, 3.6)

2. The absolute value of the coordinates are (5, 8). What are the coordinates in Quadrant II?

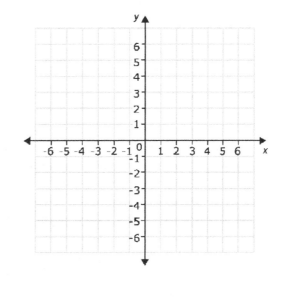

Ⓐ (−5, −8)
Ⓑ (5, −8)
Ⓒ (5, 8)
Ⓓ (−5, 8)

3. What is the absolute value of the coordinates shown on the graph?

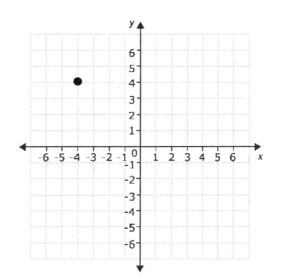

Ⓐ (−4, 4)
Ⓑ (4, 4)
Ⓒ (4, −4)
Ⓓ (−4, −4)

4. **Which of the following ordered pairs would fall in Quadrant I on the coordinate plane? Choose all that apply.**

Ⓐ (-4, 5)
Ⓑ (2, 3)
Ⓒ (2, -5)
Ⓓ (1, 1)
Ⓔ (3, 1)
Ⓕ (-3, -5)

Compare/Contrast One Author's Presentation with Another (RI.6.9)

Day 4

"Peace cannot be achieved through violence, it can only be attained through understanding." Ralph Waldo Emerson

"Peace cannot be kept by force; it can only be achieved by understanding." Albert Einstein

5. What do both of these individuals say about peace?

Ⓐ You can only have peace by fighting.
Ⓑ You can only have peace through understanding.
Ⓒ You can only have peace when everyone gets along.
Ⓓ Peace is all around us.

"Music is a world within itself, with a language we all understand." Stevie Wonder

"Without music, life would be a mistake." Fredrich Nietzsche

6. What is similar about these two quotations?

Ⓐ Both talk about languages.
Ⓑ Both talk about life.
Ⓒ Both talk about music.
Ⓓ They have nothing similar.

7. Which one of the answers below is a great way to visually compare and contrast information?

   Ⓐ Venn Diagram
   Ⓑ Chart
   Ⓒ Graph
   Ⓓ All of the above

8. Fill in the blank

   The desert is hot and dry whereas the _____ are cold and icy.

Challenge Yourself!
• Coordinate Plane
• Compare/Contrast One Author's Presentation with Another
http://www.lumoslearning.com/a/dc6-19
Day 4
See Page 7 for Signup details

Day 5

1. **Evaluate: 5^3**

   Ⓐ 15
   Ⓑ 125
   Ⓒ 8
   Ⓓ 2

2. **Write the expression using an exponent: 2 * 2 * 2 * 2 * 2 * 2**

   Ⓐ 2 * 6
   Ⓑ 12
   Ⓒ 2^6
   Ⓓ 6^2

3. **Write the expression using an exponent: y * y * y * y**

   Ⓐ 4y
   Ⓑ y/4
   Ⓒ 4^y
   Ⓓ y^4

4. **Find the numerical value of 8^4. Write your answer in standard form in the box.**

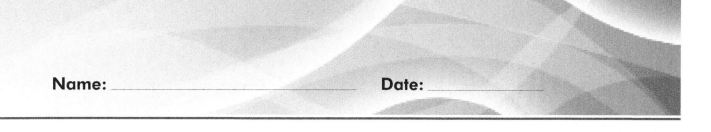
Correct Use of Adjectives and Adverbs (L.6.1.A)

Day 5

5. Identify the adjective in the following sentence.

The book that I was reading had colorful pages.

Ⓐ colorful
Ⓑ reading
Ⓒ pages
Ⓓ book

6. Identify the adjective/adjectives in the following sentence.

Earth is the most beautiful planet in the solar system.

Ⓐ Earth
Ⓑ beautiful
Ⓒ system
Ⓓ planet

7. Identify the adjective in this sentence.

The frightened alien ran back into its airship.

Ⓐ airship
Ⓑ alien
Ⓒ frightened
Ⓓ ran

8. Identify the adverb in the following sentence.

The computer printer hardly works.

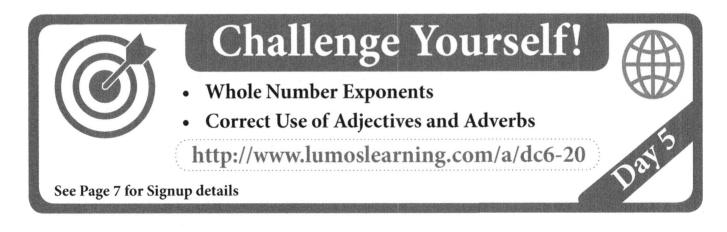

7 Tips to Hone Your Ice Hockey Skills

1. Back to Basics

"These Players...They just don't all of a sudden become skilled. From the time they were little fellas, they learned the fundamentals of the game" – Bobby Orr

As said by the great Bobby Orr, practicing the fundamentals of hockey is one of the most important things you can do. You don't just automatically become skilled; you have to work hard on the fundamental of the game and the rest will come. Yeah, it might be more exciting to run plays and learn breakout strategies, but if you still struggle with basics like skating and stick-handling, then learning more intricate skills will be a waste of time. Practice shooting, passing, and skating until they become second nature and then work on the more detailed stuff.

2. Practice off the Ice

Odds are, you don't have an ice rink in your backyard and rely on team practices to get time on the ice. On days you don't have practice, you can still train without the ice skates! Make an obstacle course with cones and try stick-handling with a tennis ball or practice sending and receiving passes. Working on these skills off of the ice will make team practices easier.

3. Don't Forget About Agility

Agility is so important in ice hockey; it helps you control your speed, make quick movements, and keep up with the fast pace of the game. Becoming more agile on the ice requires lots of practice- the more you practice making quick turns and stopping & starting, the more control you will have on the ice. You can also practice agility off of the ice by doing dot drills. To do this drill, set out dots on the ground around you, sprint to one dot and then sprint back to the starting point. Continue doing this for all of the dots, sprinting as fast as you can. This helps you practice making quick direction changes and speed control.

4.   Practice with a Purpose

Treat every practice like it is a game- shoot like it's the other team's goal and pass like there is a defender on your tail. Pretending like practice is a game will help you develop your skills in a game situation, which will make playing in the game easier.

5.   Get Tough

Ice hockey is a game all about toughness- not just physical, but mental. Mental toughness means to be resilient, to have confidence on the ice and to play like you want to win. It means using negative circumstance to motivate you to be better, rather than get you down. This is a huge skill that separates hockey players from hockey legends and, with a little practice, you can get mentally tough like the pros.

6.   Learn Some Defense

Ice hockey isn't all about the scorers- no team would be successful without skilled defensive players. When playing defense, always have your partner's back and be ready to step in should the opposing player advance. Make sure to always have your goal covered and to communicate with your team-mates. The best defensive players will be skilled at passing, backwards skating, and puck movement skills. Once you learn these skills, you're ready to dominate the defensive zone.

7.   Have Fun

The most important part of playing hockey is having fun doing it. Ice hockey should be enjoyable and you should have fun at practice and games. Sure, sometimes the game can be hard and you will be tired but that shouldn't stop you from enjoying the game. As the famous Wayne Gretzky once said, "The only way a kid is going to practice is if it's total fun for him".

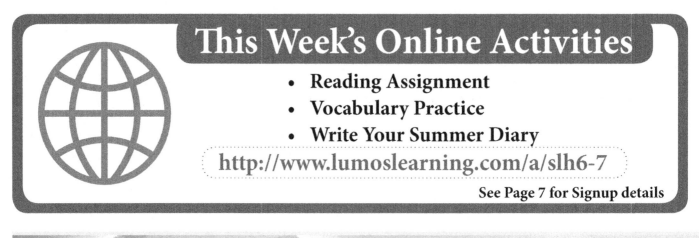

This Week's Online Activities

- Reading Assignment
- Vocabulary Practice
- Write Your Summer Diary

http://www.lumoslearning.com/a/slh6-7

See Page 7 for Signup details

Week 5 Summer Practice

Expressions Involving Variables (6.EE.A.2.A)

Day 1

1. When the expression $3(n + 7)$ is evaluated for a given value of n, the result is 33. What is the value of n?

   Ⓐ n = 4
   Ⓑ n = 5
   Ⓒ n = 21
   Ⓓ n = 120

2. Which number is acting as a coefficient in this expression? $360 + 22x - 448$

   Ⓐ 360
   Ⓑ 22
   Ⓒ 448
   Ⓓ None of these

3. Evaluate the following when n = 7: $5(n - 5)$

   Ⓐ 10
   Ⓑ −60
   Ⓒ 60
   Ⓓ 30

4. Which of the following represents the phrase "the quotient of 17 and q"? Select all the correct answers.

   Ⓐ $q \div 17$
   Ⓑ $17 \div q$
   Ⓒ $17/q$
   Ⓓ $q/17$

Day 1

5. Choose the correct pronoun to complete the sentence.

I did it by _____.

Ⓐ me
Ⓑ myself
Ⓒ I
Ⓓ my

6. Choose the correct pronoun to complete the sentence.

We _____ are responsible for the decorations.

Ⓐ us
Ⓑ ourselves
Ⓒ themselves
Ⓓ myself

7. Choose the correct pronoun to complete the sentence.

She made up the story _____ .

Ⓐ himself
Ⓑ herself
Ⓒ itself
Ⓓ themself

8. Correct the following sentence to make the referent clear.

Walking and running are more aerobic than playing team sports. They are fun, too.

Challenge Yourself!

- **Expressions Involving Variables**
- **Recognize Pronouns**

http://www.lumoslearning.com/a/dc6-21

See Page 7 for Signup details

Day 1

Identifying Expression Parts (6.EE.A.2.B)

Day 2

1. **Which of the following describes the expression 6(4−2) accurately?**

   Ⓐ Six and the difference of four and two.
   Ⓑ The product of six and the sum of four and two.
   Ⓒ The product of six and the difference of 4 and 2.
   Ⓓ The quotient of six and the difference of four and two.

2. **Which of the following best describes the expression (8 ÷2)−10?**

   Ⓐ The quotient of eight and two subtracted from ten.
   Ⓑ Ten less than the quotient of eight and two.
   Ⓒ The difference of ten and the quotient of eight and two.
   Ⓓ The product of eight and two minus ten.

3. **What are the coefficients in the expression (2x+ 15)(9x− 3)?**

   Ⓐ 2, 15, 9, −3
   Ⓑ 15, 3
   Ⓒ 15, −3
   Ⓓ 2,9

4. **Which of the following means the same as 3(2+1)? Select all the correct answers.**

   Ⓐ (2+1) + (2+1) + (2+1)
   Ⓑ 6 + 3
   Ⓒ 3 + 2 +1
   Ⓓ (6 + 1) + (6 + 1) + (6 + 1)
   Ⓔ None of the above

Day 2

Recognize and Correct Shifts in Pronoun(L.6.1.C)

5. Which pronoun best completes the following sentence?

Each student got to choose _____ own desk.

6. Which pronoun best completes the following sentence?

All the girls were excited to be able to wear _____ new dresses to the dance.

7. Fill in the blank with the correct pronoun, which best completes the following sentence?

Coach Bob was proud of the way _____ team played in the game.

8. Which pronoun best completes the following sentence?

Billy and _____ plan to ride our bikes to the park as soon as school is out.

Ⓐ I
Ⓑ me
Ⓒ us
Ⓓ his

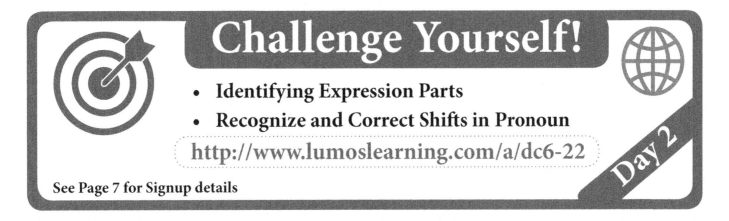

Challenge Yourself!

- **Identifying Expression Parts**
- **Recognize and Correct Shifts in Pronoun**

http://www.lumoslearning.com/a/dc6-22

See Page 7 for Signup details

Day 2

Evaluating Expressions (6.EE.A.2.C)

Day 3

1. What is the value of y in the equation $y = 3x - 13$, when $x = 6$?

    (A) 5
    (B) −4
    (C) −1
    (D) 4

2. What is the value of y in the equation $y = \frac{1}{4}x \div 2$, when $x = 32$?

    (A) 2
    (B) 4
    (C) 8
    (D) 10

3. Evaluate the following expression when $a = 3$ and $b = -8$: $3a^2 - 7b$

    (A) −44
    (B) −29
    (C) 68
    (D) 83

4. Select the equations in which $j = 7$. Choose all that apply.

    (A) $3j - 4 = 25$
    (B) $56 - j = 49$
    (C) $3j + 4 = 25$
    (D) $j^3 = 343$

Recognize and Correct Vague Pronouns (L.6.1.D)

Day 3

5. Choose the pronoun that agrees with the antecedent in the following sentence.

Anybody who forgets _____ homework will have detention at lunch.

- Ⓐ his
- Ⓑ my
- Ⓒ its
- Ⓓ their

6. Choose the pronoun that agrees with the antecedent in the following sentence.

The students made _____ own costumes for the play.

- Ⓐ her
- Ⓑ their
- Ⓒ my
- Ⓓ our

7. Choose the pronoun that agrees with the antecedent in the following sentence.

Gavin's dog follows _____ everywhere.

- Ⓐ their
- Ⓑ me
- Ⓒ his
- Ⓓ him

8. **Fill in the blank with the pronoun that agrees with the antecedent in the following sentence.**

Even though Patty is packed for the trip, _____ does not feel ready to go.

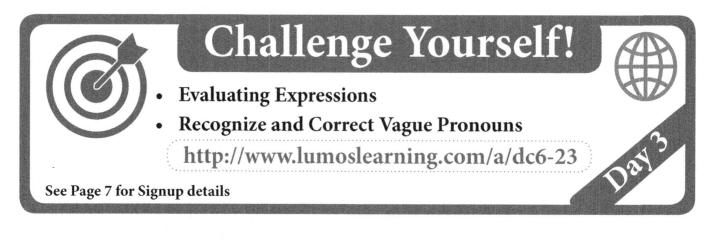

Challenge Yourself!

- **Evaluating Expressions**
- **Recognize and Correct Vague Pronouns**

http://www.lumoslearning.com/a/dc6-23

See Page 7 for Signup details

Day 3

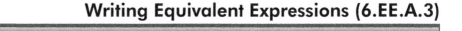

Day 4   Writing Equivalent Expressions (6.EE.A.3)

1. What is an equivalent expression for $3n - 12$?

   Ⓐ $3n + 1$
   Ⓑ $3n + 4$
   Ⓒ $3n - 4$
   Ⓓ $3(n - 4)$

2. Simplify $2n - 7n$ to create an equivalent expression.

   Ⓐ $5n$
   Ⓑ $-5n$
   Ⓒ $-n(2 - 7)$
   Ⓓ $n(5)$

3. Which expression is equivalent to $5y + 2z - 3y + z$?

   Ⓐ z
   Ⓑ $2y + 3z$
   Ⓒ yz
   Ⓓ $11yz$

4. Write the correct equation for the following expression. 3 less than the product of 4 and 5.

Recognize Variations in English (L.6.1.E)

Day 4

5. What is the correct way to write the underlined part of the following sentence?

Yesterday my mom baked cookies and we <u>eat</u> them all.

- Ⓐ will eat
- Ⓑ did eat
- Ⓒ eaten
- Ⓓ ate

6. What is the correct way to write the underlined part of the following sentence?

Jenny went to the store and <u>buy</u> apples, milk, and bread.

- Ⓐ bought
- Ⓑ will buy
- Ⓒ did buy
- Ⓓ buyed

7. What is the correct way to write the underlined part of the following sentence?

Billy and Matt rode <u>they're</u> bikes to the park.

- Ⓐ there
- Ⓑ their
- Ⓒ they
- Ⓓ them

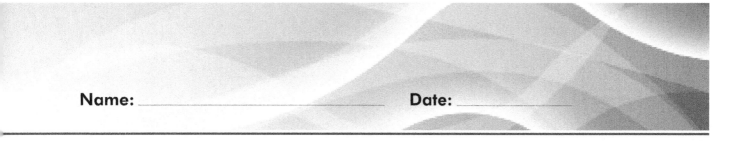
8. What is the correct way to write the underlined part of the sentence? Write your answer in the box given below.

My dog always runs <u>happy</u> by my side.

+------------------------------+
| |
| |
| |
+------------------------------+

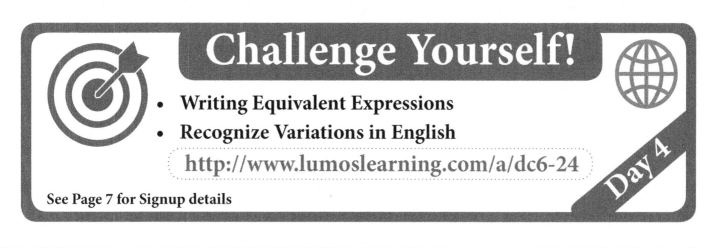

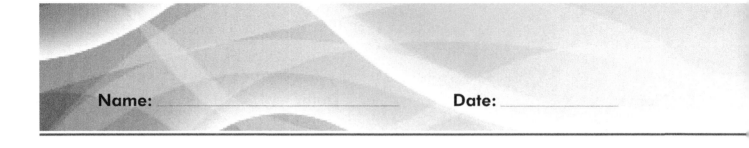
Identifying Equivalent Expressions (6.EE.A.4)

Day 5

1. **Which two expressions are equivalent?**

   Ⓐ (5/25)x and (1/3)x
   Ⓑ (5/25)x and (1/5)x
   Ⓒ (5/25)x and (1/4)x
   Ⓓ (5/25)x and (1/6)x

2. **Which two expressions are equivalent?**

   Ⓐ 7 + 21v and 2(5 + 3v)
   Ⓑ 7 + 21v and 3(4 + 7v)
   Ⓒ 7 + 21v and 7(1 + 3v)
   Ⓓ 7 + 21v and 7(7 +21v)

3. **Which two expressions are equivalent?**

   Ⓐ 32p/2 and 17p
   Ⓑ 32p/2 and 18p
   Ⓒ 32p/2 and 16p
   Ⓓ 32p/2 and 14p

4. [(8y) + (8y) + (8y)] ÷ 2 = _____ . **Simplify the expression and write the answer in the box.**

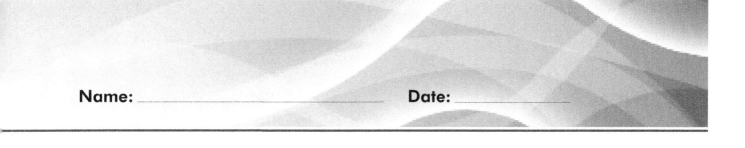

Demonstrate Command of Punctuation (L.6.2.A)

Day 5

5. Choose the answer with the correct punctuation for the sentence below.

Hi, Mom I'm home called Robby as he walked through the door

    Ⓐ "Hi, Mom! I'm home," called Robby as he walked through the door.
    Ⓑ Hi, Mom I'm home called Robby as he walked through the door.
    Ⓒ Hi Mom I'm home, called Robby as he walked through the door.
    Ⓓ Hi Mom, I'm home, called Robby, as he walked through the door.

6. Choose the answer with the correct punctuation for the sentence below.

I had bananas oranges and cherries in the refrigerator but they're all gone

    Ⓐ I had bananas oranges and cherries in the refrigerator but they're all gone.
    Ⓑ I had bananas oranges and cherries in the refrigerator, but they're all gone.
    Ⓒ I had bananas, oranges, and cherries in the refrigerator, but they're all gone.
    Ⓓ I had bananas oranges and cherries, in the refrigerator, but they're all gone.

7. Choose the answer with the correct punctuation for the sentence below.

September is the busiest month of the year that's why it's my favorite

    Ⓐ September is the busiest month of the year; that's why it's my favorite.
    Ⓑ September is the busiest month of the year that's why it's my favorite.
    Ⓒ September, is the busiest month of the year, that's why it's my favorite.
    Ⓓ September is the busiest month of the year that's why it's my favorite!

8. Rewrite the sentence below with correct punctuation.

Michelle made pizza grilled cheese and tacos for lunch but she didnt realize it was only 10:00 a.m.

Maze Game

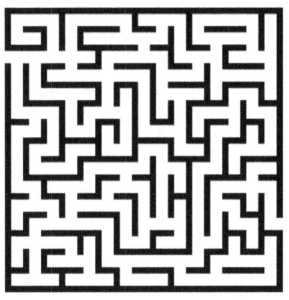

Help the beautiful kite fly out of the maze

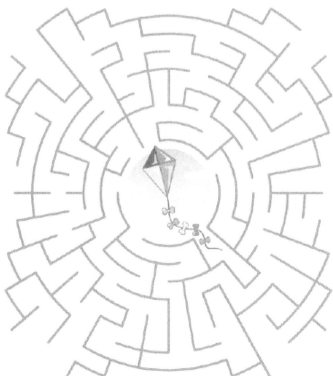

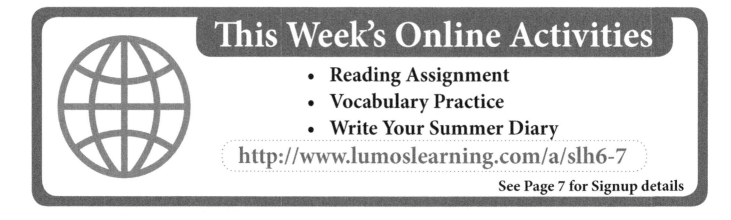

This Week's Online Activities

- Reading Assignment
- Vocabulary Practice
- Write Your Summer Diary

http://www.lumoslearning.com/a/slh6-7

See Page 7 for Signup details

Week 6 Summer Practice

Equations and Inequalities (6.EE.B.5)

Day 1

1. How many positive whole number solutions (values for x) does this inequality have?
    $x \leq 20$

    Ⓐ 19
    Ⓑ 20
    Ⓒ 21
    Ⓓ Infinite

2. Which of the following correctly shows the number sentence that the following words describe? 17 is less than or equal to the product of 6 and q.

    Ⓐ $17 \leq 6q$
    Ⓑ $17 \leq 6 - q$
    Ⓒ $17 < 6q$
    Ⓓ $17 \geq 6q$

3. Which of the following correctly shows the number sentence that the following words describe? The quotient of *d* and *5* is 15.

    Ⓐ $\dfrac{5}{d} = 15$

    Ⓑ $5d = 15$

    Ⓒ $\dfrac{d}{5} = 15$

    Ⓓ $d - 5 = 15$

4. Select all values that could correctly represent b in the equation.
    3b + 2 < 15

    Ⓐ 1
    Ⓑ 2
    Ⓒ 4
    Ⓓ 5
    Ⓔ 7

Correct Spelling (L.6.2.B)

Day 1

5. Choose the correct word that fits the blank:

Grind the wheat to a powdery _____.

   Ⓐ flower
   Ⓑ flour
   Ⓒ floor
   Ⓓ floure

6. Choose the correct word that fits the blank:

Among all _____, my favorite is the pink rose.

   Ⓐ floors
   Ⓑ flour
   Ⓒ flowers
   Ⓓ floures

7. Choose the correct word that fits the blank:

The last _____ creaked as I stepped on to it.

   Ⓐ stare
   Ⓑ stair
   Ⓒ steer
   Ⓓ stiar

8. What do you call a proposed route of travel and a guidebook for a journey?

_____

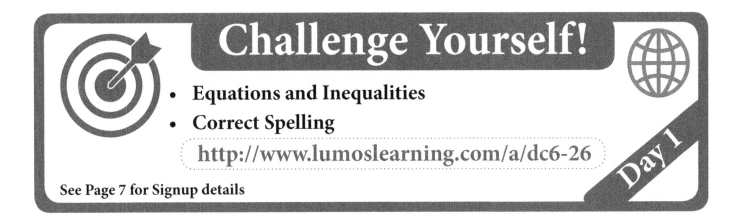

Challenge Yourself!

- Equations and Inequalities
- Correct Spelling

http://www.lumoslearning.com/a/dc6-26

See Page 7 for Signup details

Day 1

Modeling with Expressions (6.EE.B.6)

Day 2

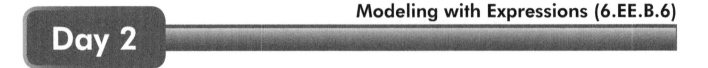

1. Roula had 117 gumballs. Amy had x less than 1/2 the amount that Roula had. Which expression shows how many gumballs Amy had?

    Ⓐ 117 − x/2
    Ⓑ (1/2)(117) − x.
    Ⓒ 117 − 2x
    Ⓓ 2x + 117

2. Benny earned $20.00 for weeding the garden. He also earned c dollars for mowing the lawn. Then he spent x dollars at the candy store. Which expression best represents this situation?

    Ⓐ $20 − c − x
    Ⓑ $20 + c − x
    Ⓒ $20 + c + x
    Ⓓ $20 + x/c

3. Clinton loves to cook. He makes a total of 23 different items. Clinton makes 6 different desserts, 12 appetizers, and x main courses. Which equation represents the total amount of food that Clinton cooked?

    Ⓐ 6 − 12 + x = 23
    Ⓑ 6 + 12 + x = 23
    Ⓒ 18 − x = 23
    Ⓓ 6 + 12 − x = 23

4. Choose the box(es) that demonstrate that x is a number greater than 5. Choose all that apply.

    Ⓐ x < 5
    Ⓑ x > 5
    Ⓒ x + 5
    Ⓓ x - 5
    Ⓔ 5 < x

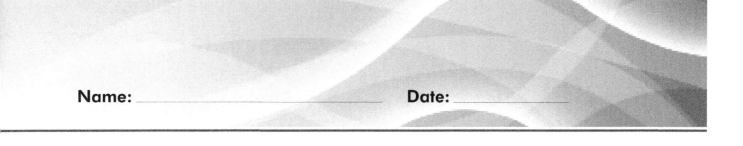

Vary Sentences (L.6.3.A)

Day 2

5. What is the best way to combine the following sentences?

The oven temperature was too hot. The cookies got burnt.

- Ⓐ The oven temperature was too hot, the cookies got burnt.
- Ⓑ The oven temperature was too hot because the cookies got burnt.
- Ⓒ The oven temperature was too hot the cookies got burnt.
- Ⓓ The oven temperature was too hot, so the cookies got burnt.

6. What is the best way to combine the following sentences?

Mike and Johnny wanted to play outside. It was raining so they couldn't.

- Ⓐ Mike and Johnny wanted to play outside, but it was raining.
- Ⓑ Because of the rain, Mike and Johnny couldn't play outside.
- Ⓒ Mike and Johnny wanted to play outside and it was raining so they couldn't.
- Ⓓ Mike and Johnny wanted to play outside in the rain.

7. What is the best way to combine the following sentences?

We should go to the mall. After school.

- Ⓐ After school, we should go to the mall.
- Ⓑ We should go to the mall, after school.
- Ⓒ We should go to the mall, and after school.
- Ⓓ After school, to the mall we should go.

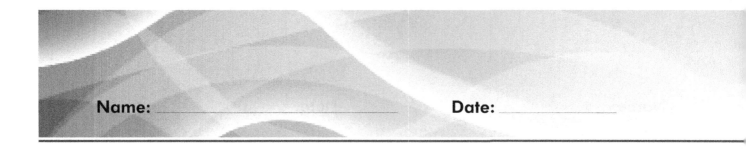
8. **Which is the best way to combine the following sentences? Circle the correct answer choice**

The puppy was soft and cuddly. It was brown.

Ⓐ The puppy was soft and cuddly, and it was brown.
Ⓑ The brown puppy was soft and cuddly.
Ⓒ The puppy was soft and cuddly and brown.
Ⓓ The puppy was brown and it was soft and it was cuddly.

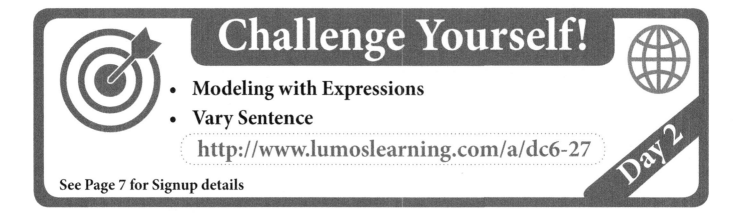

Challenge Yourself!

- **Modeling with Expressions**
- **Vary Sentence**

http://www.lumoslearning.com/a/dc6-27

See Page 7 for Signup details

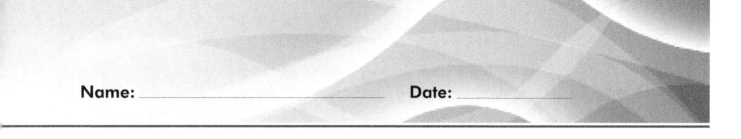

Solving One-Step Equations (6.EE.B.7)

Day 3

1. Which of the following equations describes this function?

X	Y
13	104
17	136
20	160
9	72

Ⓐ y = 18x
Ⓑ y = x + 4
Ⓒ y = x + 32
Ⓓ y = 8x

2. What is the value of x?

$$-7x = 56$$

Ⓐ x = −7
Ⓑ x = 8
Ⓒ x = −49
Ⓓ x = −8

3. Does this table show a linear relationship between x and y?

X	Y
13	169
15	225
12	144
	400
16	
7	
	64

(A) yes
(B) no
(C) yes, but only when x is positive
(D) yes, but only when y is a perfect square

4. Select the equations in which k = 8. Select all the correct answers.

(A) 3(6 + k) = 42
(B) ((4) 7) / k = 14
(C) 8k – 4 = 60
(D) 7(k / 2) = 35

Maintain Consistency in Style and Tone (L.6.3.B)

Day 3

5. Which of the following sentences paints the clearest picture?

(A) Even though the sun was shining, Mary couldn't help but feel chilled by the cool morning breeze.
(B) Even though the sun was shining, Mary was still cold.
(C) The sun was shining but the breeze made Mary cold.
(D) Mary was chilled on the sunny, yet breeze morning.

6. **Which of the following sentences uses the most descriptive words and style?**

   Ⓐ As the darkness fell, Scott was scared of what might be out there.
   Ⓑ As the darkness fell, Scott couldn't help but be weary of what might lurk out there in the shadows.
   Ⓒ As the darkness fell, Scott was frightened by what he could not see.
   Ⓓ Scott is scared of the dark.

7. **Which of the following sentences provides the most detail about the topic?**

   Ⓐ Callie loved the smell of cookies.
   Ⓑ Callie loved the smell of her mother's cookies.
   Ⓒ Callie loved the smell of her mother's fresh baked cookies.
   Ⓓ Callie loved the smell of her mother's fresh baked chocolate chip cookies.

8. **Which of the following sentences is the most concise? Circle the correct answer choice.**

   Ⓐ Beth thought the test was hard and difficult. Mary thought the test was easy.
   Ⓑ While Beth thought the test was challenging, Mary thought it was easy.
   Ⓒ Beth thought the test was hard and Mary thought it was easy.
   Ⓓ Beth thought the test was hard and difficult, but Mary thought the test was easy.

Challenge Yourself!

- **Solving One-Step Problems**
- **Maintain Consistency in Style and Tone**

  http://www.lumoslearning.com/a/dc6-28

Day 3

See Page 7 for Signup details

Representing Inequalities (6.EE.B.8)

Day 4

1. A second grade class raised caterpillars. They had 12 caterpillars. Less than half of the caterpillars turned into butterflies. Which inequality shows how many caterpillars turned into butterflies?

   (A) $x < 6$
   (B) $x > 6$
   (C) $x \le 6$
   (D) $x \ge 6$

2. Elliot has at least 5 favorite foods. How many favorite foods could Elliot have?

   (A) 4
   (B) 2
   (C) none
   (D) an infinite number

3. Julie has a box full of crayons. Her box of crayons has 549 crayons and at least 8 of them are red. Which inequality represents how many crayons could be red?

   (A) $x \ge 549$
   (B) $8 \ge x \ge 549$
   (C) $8 \ge x$
   (D) $8 \le x \le 549$

4. Choose the box that best represents the inequality on the line below.

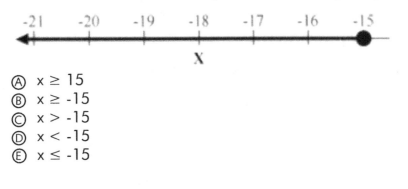

   (A) $x \ge 15$
   (B) $x \ge -15$
   (C) $x > -15$
   (D) $x < -15$
   (E) $x \le -15$

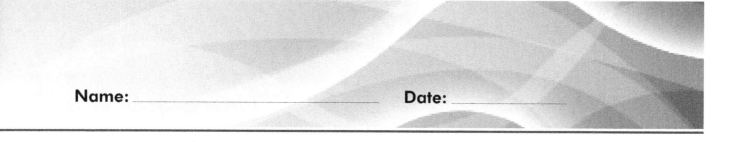
Use Context Clues to Determine Word Meaning (L.6.4.A)

Day 4

Julio was happy and astounded when he won MVP for the soccer season. He had been sure that Reuben or Carlos were going to be chosen.

5. The word "astounded" in this context means: _____.

Ⓐ disappointed
Ⓑ very surprised
Ⓒ satisfied
Ⓓ pleased

A spider web may look flimsy, but spider silk is actually five times stronger than steel. It is tougher, stronger, and more flexible than anything humans have been able to produce.

6. The word "flimsy" in this context means: _____.

Ⓐ beautiful
Ⓑ silky
Ⓒ weak
Ⓓ inflexible

The sweltering summer heat made the beach unpleasant.

7. In the above context, "sweltering" means _____

Ⓐ cold
Ⓑ frigid
Ⓒ hot
Ⓓ humid

The big, nasty creature was brown and hairy; it looked hideous.

8. In the above context, "hideous" means _____

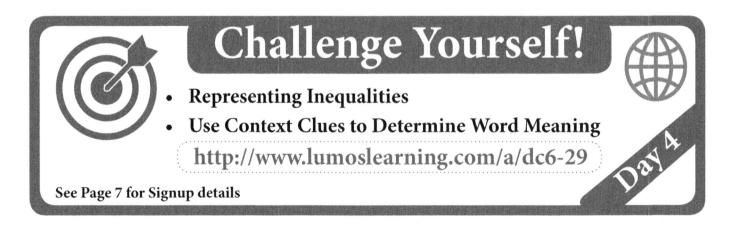

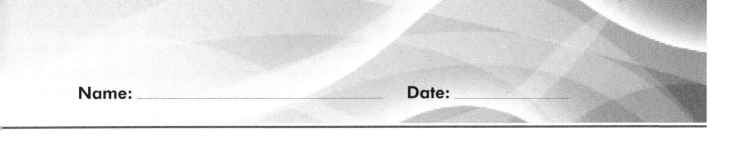

Day 5

Quantitative Relationships (6.EE.C.9)

1. Logan loves candy! He goes to the store and sees that the bulk candy is $0.79 a pound. Logan wants to buy p pounds of candy and needs to know how much money (m) he needs. Which equation would be used to figure out how much money Logan needs?

   Ⓐ $m = 0.79 \div p$
   Ⓑ $m = 0.79(p)$
   Ⓒ $0.79 = m(p)$
   Ⓓ $m = 0.79 + p$

2. Logan loves candy! He goes to the store and sees that the bulk candy is $0.84 a pound. Logan wants to buy 3 pounds of candy. Using the equation m = 0.84(p), figure out how much money (m) Logan needs.

   Ⓐ $1.68
   Ⓑ $2.52
   Ⓒ $2.25
   Ⓓ $2.54

3. Norman is going on a road trip. He has to purchase gas so that he can make it to his first destination. Gas is $3.55 a gallon. Norman gets g gallons. Which equation would Norman use to figure out how much money (t) it cost to get the gas?

   Ⓐ $t = g(3.55)$
   Ⓑ $t = g \div 3.55$
   Ⓒ $t = 3.55 \div g$
   Ⓓ $t = g + 3.55$

4. Sodas cost $1.25 at the vending machine. Complete the table to show the quantity and total cost of sodas purchased.

Day	Money Spent on Sodas	Sodas Purchased	Price per Soda
Monday		24	$1.25
Wednesday	$57.50		$1.25
Friday	$41.25		$1.25

Use Common Roots and Affixes (L.6.4.B)

Day 5

5. Which of the following is a true statement?

Ⓐ A suffix or ending is an affix, which is placed at the end of a word.
Ⓑ A prefix or beginning is an affix, which is placed at the beginning of a word.
Ⓒ A suffix is attached at the beginning of the word.
Ⓓ Both A and B

6. When the suffix "-able" is added to the word "cap", it means-

Ⓐ able to do something
Ⓑ to do anything
Ⓒ not able to do something
Ⓓ not able to do anything

7. Identify the suffix in the following words:

Salvage, Storage, Forage

Ⓐ A
Ⓑ ge
Ⓒ age
Ⓓ rage

8. Identify the meaning of the root word in the following words:

Recede, secede, precede

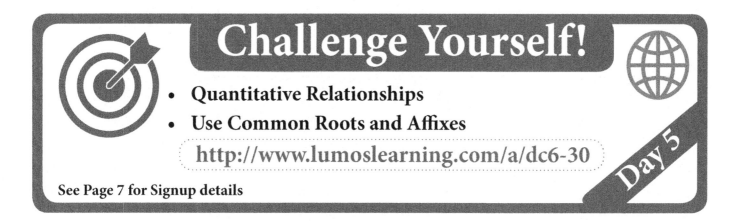

Summer Learning Activity Videos

Use the link below or QR code to watch the videos

http://lumoslearning.com/a/summervideos

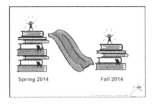

Beating the Summer Academic Loss

Beating the Brain Drain through Literacy

Beating the Brain Drain through Computing

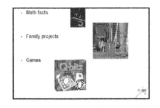

Warm-Up to a Great School Year

This Week's Online Activities

- Reading Assignment
- Vocabulary Practice
- Write Your Summer Diary

http://www.lumoslearning.com/a/slh6-7

See Page 7 for Signup details

Week 7 Summer Practice

Area (6.G.A.1)

Day 1

1. **What is the area of the figure below?**

   Ⓐ 16 square units
   Ⓑ 63 square units
   Ⓒ 32 square units
   Ⓓ 45 square units

2. **What is the area of the figure below?**

   Ⓐ 12 square units
   Ⓑ 24 square units
   Ⓒ 18 square units
   Ⓓ 36 square units

3. **What is the area of the figure below? (Assume that the vertical height of the parallelogram is 3 units .)**

   7
   4

   Ⓐ 28 square units
   Ⓑ 12 square units
   Ⓒ 14 square units
   Ⓓ 21 square units

4. **Calculate the area of the triangle shown. Write the answer in the box given below.**

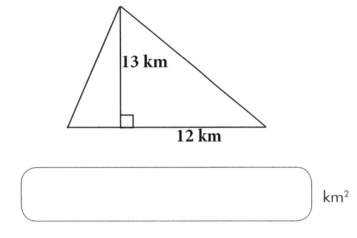

13 km

12 km

```
┌─────────────────────────────┐
│                             │   km²
└─────────────────────────────┘
```

Consult Reference Materials (L.6.4.C)

Day 1

5. Alphabetize the following words:

hibiscus, petunia, rose, honeysuckle, daffodil

ⓐ hibiscus, petunia, rose, honeysuckle, daffodil
ⓑ daffodil, hibiscus, honeysuckle, petunia, rose
ⓒ daffodil, honeysuckle, hibiscus, petunia, rose
ⓓ hibiscus, petunia, rose, daffodil, honeysuckle

6. Alphabetize the following words:

mouse, mule, monkey, moose, mole

ⓐ mouse, monkey, moose, mole, mule
ⓑ mouse, mule, monkey, moose, mole
ⓒ mouse, moose, monkey, mole, mule
ⓓ mole, monkey, moose, mouse, mule

7. Alphabetize the following words:

sustain, solicit, sizzle, sanitize, secure

Ⓐ sustain, solicit, sizzle, sanitize, secure
Ⓑ sanitize, secure, sustain, solicit, sizzle
Ⓒ sanitize, solicit, sizzle, sustain, secure
Ⓓ sanitize, secure, sizzle, solicit, sustain

8. How many syllables are in the word "organized?"

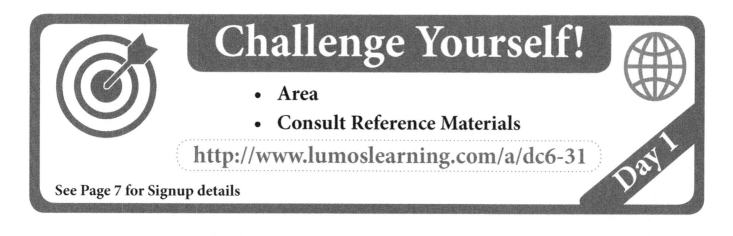

Challenge Yourself!

- Area
- Consult Reference Materials

http://www.lumoslearning.com/a/dc6-31

Day 1

See Page 7 for Signup details

Surface Area and Volume (6.G.A.2)

Day 2

1. How many rectangular faces would a trapezoidal prism have?

   Ⓐ two
   Ⓑ four
   Ⓒ six
   Ⓓ zero

2. Which of the following statements is true of a rhombus?

   Ⓐ A rhombus is a parallelogram.
   Ⓑ A rhombus is a quadrilateral.
   Ⓒ A rhombus is equilateral.
   Ⓓ All of the above are true.

3. A cube has a volume of 1,000 cm³. What is its surface area?

   Ⓐ 100 sq. cm
   Ⓑ 60 sq. cm
   Ⓒ 600 sq. cm
   Ⓓ It cannot be determined.

4. Determine the volume of the prism shown. Write your answer in the box given below.

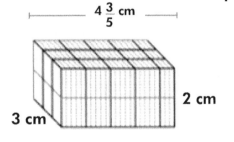

cm³

Day 2   Determine the Meaning of a Word (L.6.4.D)

5. What does the underlined word in the sentence mean?

Johnny was certain he hadn't <u>misplaced</u> his glove but he couldn't find it.

- (A) found
- (B) lost
- (C) hid
- (D) borrowed

6. What does the underlined word in the sentence mean?

Despite the <u>brisk</u> temperatures, football fans still packed the stadium to watch the championship game.

- (A) hot
- (B) fast
- (C) cool
- (D) exciting

7. What does the underlined word in the sentence mean?

Natalie and Sophia couldn't wait to ride the roller coaster. They'd heard it was very <u>exhilarating</u>.

- (A) fast
- (B) frightening
- (C) exciting
- (D) boring

8. What does the underlined word in the sentence mean? Circle the correct answer choice.

The whimpering puppies were clearly <u>ravenous</u>. They devoured the food when it was ready.

Ⓐ hungry
Ⓑ sleepy
Ⓒ playful
Ⓓ scared

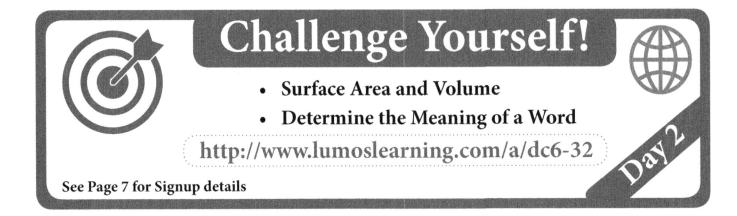

Challenge Yourself!

- Surface Area and Volume
- Determine the Meaning of a Word

http://www.lumoslearning.com/a/dc6-32

See Page 7 for Signup details

Day 2

Coordinate Geometry (6.G.A.3)

Day 3

1. The points A (0, 0), B (5, 0), C (6, 2), D (5, 5), and E (0, 5) are plotted in a coordinate grid. Describe the angles in pentagon ABCDE.

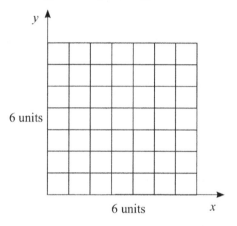

Ⓐ 2 right angles and 3 obtuse angles
Ⓑ 2 right angles, 2 obtuse angles, and 1 acute angle
Ⓒ 3 right angles and 2 obtuse angles
Ⓓ 2 right angles, 2 acute angles, and 1 obtuse angle

2. The corners of a shape are located at (1,2), (5,2), (2,3) and (4,3) in a coordinate grid. What type of shape is it?

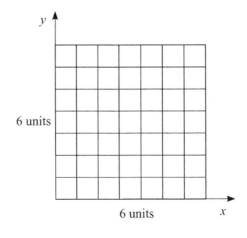

Ⓐ square
Ⓑ parallelogram
Ⓒ rhombus
Ⓓ trapezoid

3. Which of the following graphs shows a 180 degree clockwise rotation about the origin?

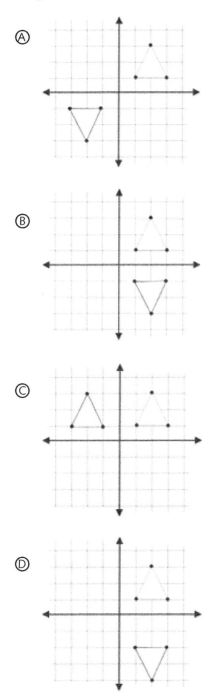

Ⓐ

Ⓑ

Ⓒ

Ⓓ

4. **What is the area of the rectangle. Write your answer in the box given below.**

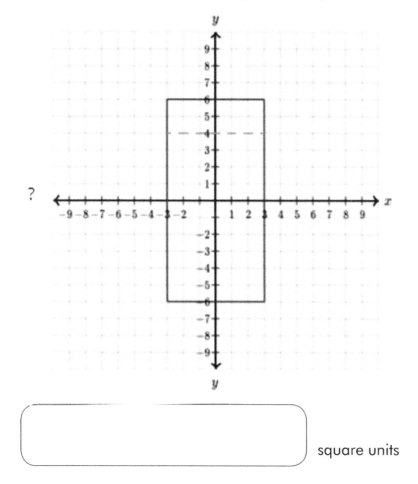

square units

Interpret Figures of Speech (L.6.5.A)

Day 3

5. **What type(s) of figurative language is(are) being used in the sentence below?**

Jimmy and Johnny jumped like jelly beans.

   Ⓐ Metaphor
   Ⓑ Idiom
   Ⓒ Personification
   Ⓓ Alliteration

6. **What type of figurative language is being used in the sentence below?**

Don't spill the beans.

- Ⓐ Idiom
- Ⓑ Onomatopoeia
- Ⓒ Personification
- Ⓓ Alliteration

7. **What type of figurative language is being used in the sentence below?**

That sandwich is as big as a car.

- Ⓐ Personification
- Ⓑ Simile
- Ⓒ Metaphor
- Ⓓ Alliteration

8. **What type of figurative language is being used in the sentence below? Enter your answer in the box given below**

Stop pulling my leg.

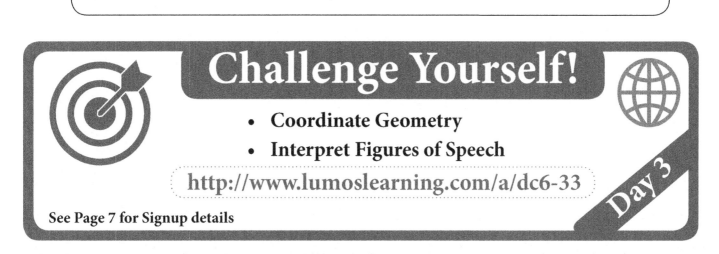

Challenge Yourself!

- **Coordinate Geometry**
- **Interpret Figures of Speech**

http://www.lumoslearning.com/a/dc6-33

Day 3

See Page 7 for Signup details

Nets (6.G.A.4)

Day 4

1. Identify the solid given its net:

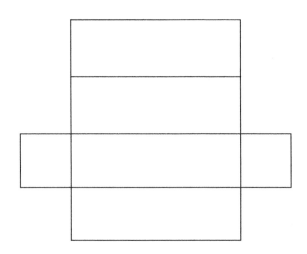

- Ⓐ Rectangular prism
- Ⓑ Cube
- Ⓒ Triangular prism
- Ⓓ Sphere

2. Identify the solid given its net:

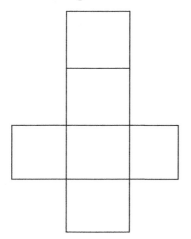

- Ⓐ Cube
- Ⓑ Sphere
- Ⓒ Rectangular prism
- Ⓓ Square pyramid

3. Identify the solid given its net:

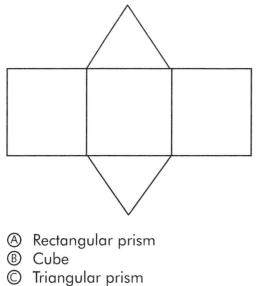

- Ⓐ Rectangular prism
- Ⓑ Cube
- Ⓒ Triangular prism
- Ⓓ Sphere

4. Use a net or formula to find the surface area of the figure. The length is 5, the width is 4 and the height is 2. Write your answer in the box given below.

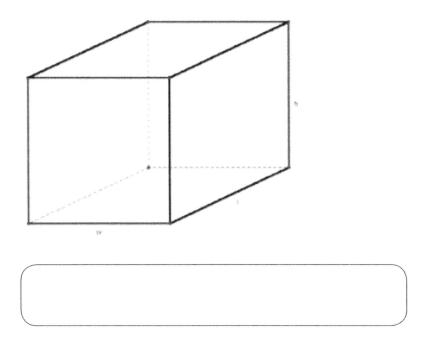

Use Relationships to Better Understand Words (L.6.5.B)

Day 4

5. Identify the cause and the effect in the following sentence:

The blizzard was so widespread that all flights were cancelled.

cause _____ effect _____

    Ⓐ   cause-blizzard; effect- flights cancelled
    Ⓑ   cause-flights; effect- blizzard
    Ⓒ   cause-blizzard; effect- flights
    Ⓓ   cause-cancelled flights; effect- widespread blizzard

6. Identify the cause and the effect in the following sentence:

Several hundred people were left homeless by the flood.

cause _____ effect _____

    Ⓐ cause- homeless people; effect -flood
    Ⓑ cause- flood; effect - people left homeless
    Ⓒ cause- people; effect -homeless
    Ⓓ cause- flood; effect -several hundred people

7. Identify the cause and the effect in the following sentence:

Pedro's friendly attitude got him the job.

cause _____ effect _____

    Ⓐ cause- Pedro; effect- friendly attitude
    Ⓑ cause- Pedro; effect- got the job
    Ⓒ cause- friendly attitude; effect- got the job
    Ⓓ cause- job; effect- friendly attitude

8. Identify the cause and the effect in the following sentence:

Whistling while you work makes the task easier.

cause _____ effect _____

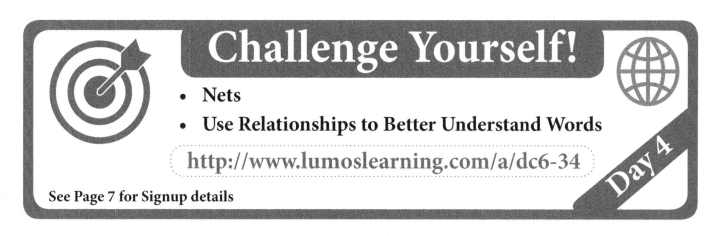

Challenge Yourself!

- **Nets**
- **Use Relationships to Better Understand Words**

http://www.lumoslearning.com/a/dc6-34

Day 4

See Page 7 for Signup details

Day 5

1. The chart below shows the participation of a sixth grade class in its school's music activities. Each student was allowed to pick one music activity.

    How many boys are in the sixth grade?

    ### Music Activity Participation

    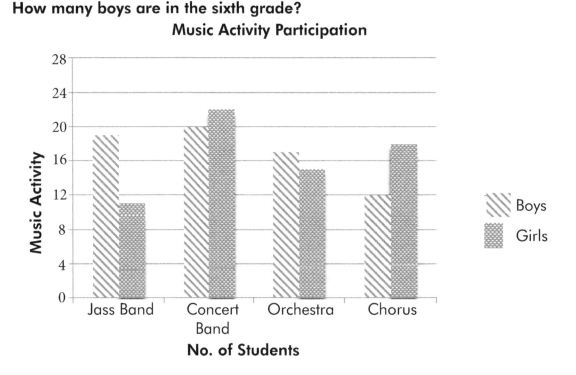

    Ⓐ 86
    Ⓑ 68
    Ⓒ 42
    Ⓓ 12

2. **A student wanted to know what the sixth grade girls' favorite song was. What would be the best way to conduct a survey?**

    Ⓐ Do an internet search of favorite songs of young girls.
    Ⓑ Survey the sixth grade boys.
    Ⓒ Survey the sixth grade girls.
    Ⓓ Conduct a survey at the mall.

3. **Emily wanted to know what the range of daily temperatures this past week was. What would be the best way of conducting her survey?**

    Ⓐ Take the temperature once during the week.
    Ⓑ Take the temperature only in the morning.
    Ⓒ Take the temperature only in the evening.
    Ⓓ Take the temperature two times a day, at the warmest and coolest times of the day.

4. **Select the questions that qualify as statistical questions. Choose all that apply.**

    Ⓐ How many letters are in my last name?
    Ⓑ How many letters are in the last names of the students in my 6th grade class?
    Ⓒ What are the colors of the shoes worn by the students in my school?
    Ⓓ What are the heart rates of the students in a 6th grade class?
    Ⓔ How many hours of sleep per night do 6th graders usually get when they have school the next day?

Distinguish Between Word Associations and Definitions (L.6.5.C)

Day 5

5. **Denotation of a word is the _____.**

    Ⓐ slang for a word.
    Ⓑ literal meaning.
    Ⓒ part of speech of a word.
    Ⓓ feelings we have about a word.

6. Connotation refers to _____.

Ⓐ the literal meaning of a word.
Ⓑ the part of speech of a word.
Ⓒ how we feel about a word.
Ⓓ the slang meaning of a word.

7. Which of the following words has the same denotative meaning as the word house?

Ⓐ dwelling
Ⓑ abode
Ⓒ residence
Ⓓ All of the above

The word "old" has a negative connotation.

8. Which of the following words has the same denotation but a positive connotation? Circle the correct answer choice

Ⓐ Decrepit
Ⓑ Ancient
Ⓒ Elderly
Ⓓ Over the hill

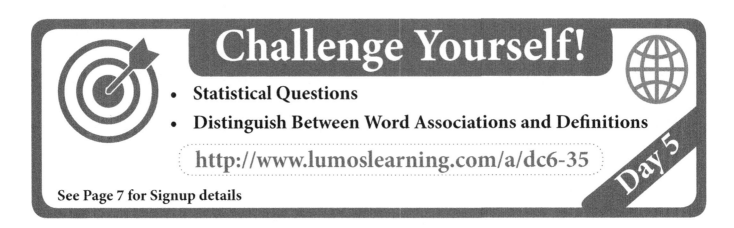

Challenge Yourself!

• Statistical Questions
• Distinguish Between Word Associations and Definitions

http://www.lumoslearning.com/a/dc6-35

Day 5

See Page 7 for Signup details

Word Games

UNDERWATER WORLD

S	S	H	A	S	H	C	R	A	B
T	I	S	R	K	E	L	L	N	A
G	N	E	A	H	O	D	O	C	E
R	A	Y	L	O	R	O	L	P	H
S	Q	U	S	B	S	H	W	H	I
T	D	I	T	O	E	S	L	A	N
U	R	T	E	C	F	I	E	L	R
J	E	L	R	T	O	P	U	A	E
E	S	E	A	B	E	D	S	R	E
L	L	Y	F	I	S	H	C	O	F

ANEMONE
COD
CORAL REEF
CRAB
DOLPHIN
FISH
FLYING FISH
HALIBUT
HERRING
JELLYFISH
LOBSTER
MORAY EEL
MUSSEL
OCEAN
OCTOPUS

OYSTER
PLANKTON
SALMON
SCUBA DIVING
SEABED
SEAHORSE
SEAWEED
SHARK
SHELL
SQUID
STARFISH
STINGRAY
TURTLE
URCHIN
WHALE

S	A	L	M	A	N	E	M	E	T
S	M	O	O	P	N	K	O	N	U
T	A	R	N	L	A	T	O	N	B
S	R	A	Y	U	R	M	L	E	I
C	F	I	E	E	C	U	S	S	L
U	B	S	H	L	H	I	N	H	A
C	A	D	I	V	O	T	E	R	D
O	D	G	N	I	Y	S	G	S	E
F	I	N	H	S	E	H	N	E	E
L	Y	G	F	I	R	R	I	A	W

HAPPY HALLOWEEN!

I	R	T	H	C	T	I	W	E	S
C	B	A	T	F	U	L	L	M	U
K	F	J	P	U	M	N	O	O	O
O	A	E	N	O	P	T	E	D	H
R	L	L	A	C	K	N	U	A	H
T	L	L	E	T	I	R	E	D	T
R	E	Y	B	O	N	S	P	I	S
C	A	O	W	B	E	R	G	H	O
H	T	R	C	E	R	A	C	S	C
I	L	D	R	E	N	Y	D	N	A

AUTUMN
BAT
BLACK CAT
BROOMSTICK
CANDY
CANDY CORN
CHILDREN
COSTUME PARTY
FALL
FULL MOON
GHOST
HAUNTED HOUSE
HORROW FILM

JACK-O-LANTERN
JELLY BEAN
MUMMY
OCTOBER
PUMPKIN
SAMHAIN
SCARE CROW
SKELETON
SPIDER
SPOOKY
TRICK OR TREAT
VAMPIRE
WITCH

C	A	N	E	R	I	P	M	A	N
U	M	D	Y	C	O	R	N	V	O
T	E	M	U	M	C	K	O	S	T
S	P	N	B	M	A	T	L	K	E
O	A	I	L	Y	J	A	A	E	L
C	R	A	A	C	K	C	N	N	H
S	T	H	B	N	R	E	T	M	O
P	Y	M	R	M	A	U	T	U	R
O	Y	A	O	L	I	F	W	O	R
O	K	S	O	M	S	T	I	C	K

MERRY CHRISTMAS!

Word List (first puzzle):
BAUBLES
CANDY CANE
CAROLS
CHRISTMAS LIGHTS
CHRISTMAS TREE
DECEMBER
ELVES
GIFTS
GINGERBREAD
GREETING CARDS
HOLLY

MISTLETOE
NORTH POLE
NUTCRACKER
ORNAMENTS
POINSETTIA
REINDEER
ROBIN
SANTA CLAUS
SNOWFLAKES
SNOWMAN
TOY FACTORY
WINTER

Find and cross out all the listed words. The words may go horizontally, vertically, diagonally, not backwards. The remaining letters will spell a secret message.

AKEPA	PETREL
AKIALOA	PRINIA
ARGUS	QUAIL
BOBOLINK	RAVEN
BUSTARD	SCAUP
CRAKE	SPARROW
CUTIA	STINT
DOVEKIE	STORK
DRONGO	VERDIN
DUNLIN	VIREO
EIDER	
FIGBIRD	
FINCH	
GIANT SNIPE	
KAKAPO	
KAMAO	
KILLDEER	
MONAL	
MOURNER	
NODDY	

```
A R G U S T R H E O N C
K I L L D E E R P E O N
E P R I N I A A V S T W
P E L R L A K A T I O R
A B U S T A R D O R E N
D O V E K I E V R D T U
M C Q A E H N A I A I S
N A U K C M P E T R E L
G I A N T S N I P E E B
S R I O F N D R O N G O
C F L D I E D A M C K B
A F T D G E R T O U A O
U H R Y B S T I N T M L
P E A K I A L O A I A I
V S T O R K E T L A O N
O U C A D U N L I N N K
```

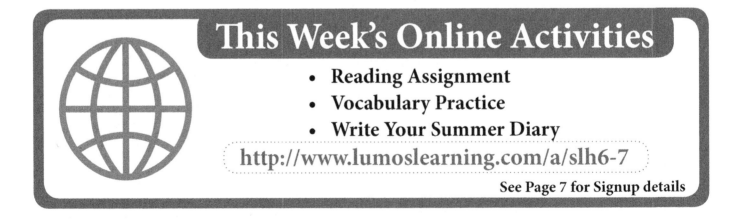

Week 8 Summer Practice

Distribution (6.SP.A.2)

Day 1

1. If the total sales for socks was $60, what is the best estimate for the total sales of pants?

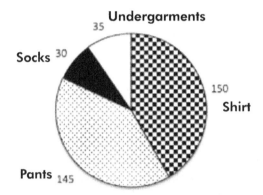

Note: Data represent the angles for each category

- Ⓐ $200
- Ⓑ $300
- Ⓒ $60
- Ⓓ $1,000

2. The sixth graders at Kilmer Middle School can choose to participate in one of the four music activities offered. The number of students participating in each activity is shown in the bar graph below. Use the information shown to respond to the following: How many sixth graders are in the Jazz Band?

Music Activity Participation

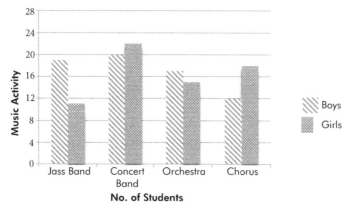

(A) 19 sixth graders
(B) 20 sixth graders
(C) 30 sixth graders
(D) 25 sixth graders

3. A .J. has downloaded 400 songs onto his computer. The songs are from a variety of genres. The circle graph below shows the breakdown (by genre) of his collection. Use the information shown to respond to the following: About how many more R + B songs than rock songs has A.J. downloaded

A.J.'s Music Collections

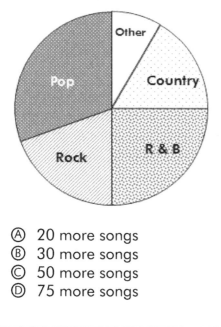

(A) 20 more songs
(B) 30 more songs
(C) 50 more songs
(D) 75 more songs

4. The height of the four tallest downtown buildings from three different cities is given in the table below. Calculate the mean height of each city's buildings and match it with the correct answer from the bottom table.

City A Buildings	Height (m)
1	23
2	32
3	35
4	45

City B Buildings	Height (m)
1	15
2	22
3	28
4	25

City C Buildings	Height (m)
1	15
2	30
3	35
4	36

	22.50 m	29 m	23.20 m	33.75 m	18 m
City A Buildings	O	O	O	O	O
City B Buildings	O	O	O	O	O
City C Buildings	O	O	O	O	O

Use Grade Appropriate Words (L.6.6)

Day 1

The word "racket" has multiple meanings.

5. **Which sentence uses the word "racket" where it means "noise?"**

Ⓐ I nearly forgot my racket before tennis practice.
Ⓑ There was a lot of racket coming from my brother's room.
Ⓒ My racket broke when I dropped it down the stairs.
Ⓓ I hope I get a new racket for my birthday.

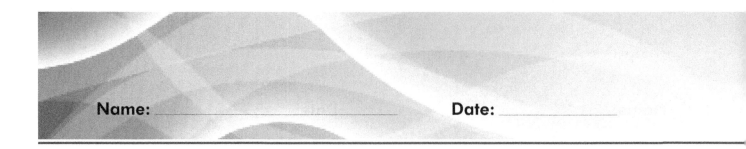

The word "bear" has multiple meanings.

6. Which sentence uses the word "bear" where it means "to hold up?"

Ⓐ The baby bear is so cute!
Ⓑ I cannot bear to see someone hurt.
Ⓒ That apple tree sure does bear a lot of fruit.
Ⓓ I can't bear to stand on my broken ankle.

The word "patient" has multiple meanings.

7. Which sentence uses the word "patient" where it means "quietly waiting?"

Ⓐ The doctor sent the patient for x-rays of her wrist.
Ⓑ The nurse checked on the patient frequently.
Ⓒ The little boy is being very patient in line.
Ⓓ The patient needs to go home and rest before he feels better.

8. Which of the following words best completes the sentence? Circle the correct answer choice

The team was very _____ about practicing.

Ⓐ lazy
Ⓑ sloppy
Ⓒ successful
Ⓓ diligent

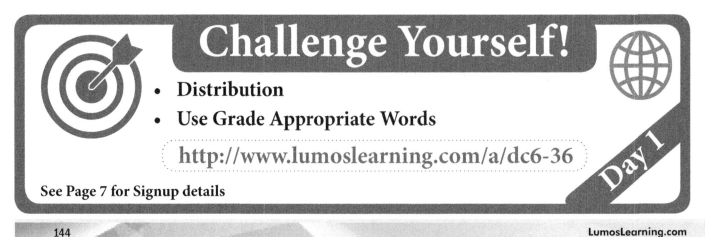

Challenge Yourself!

- **Distribution**
- **Use Grade Appropriate Words**

http://www.lumoslearning.com/a/dc6-36

Day 1

See Page 7 for Signup details

Central Tendency (6.SP.A.3)

Day 2

1 Jason was conducting a scientific experiment using bean plants. He measured the height (in centimeters) of each plant after three weeks. These were his measurements (in cm): 12, 15, 11, 17, 19, 21, 13, 11, 16

What is the average (mean) height? What is the median height?

Ⓐ Mean = 15 cm, Median = 19 cm
Ⓑ Mean = 15 cm, Median = 15 cm
Ⓒ Mean = 19 cm, Median = 15 cm
Ⓓ Mean = 15 cm, Median = 13 cm

2. Stacy has 60 pairs of shoes. She has shoes that have a heel height of between 1 inch and 4 inches. Stacy has 20 pairs of shoes that have a 1 inch heel, 15 pairs of shoes that have a 2 inch heel and 20 pairs of shoes that have a 3 inch heel height. Remaining shoes have 4 inch heel height. What is the average heel height of all 60 pairs of Stacy's shoes?

Ⓐ 1.3 inches
Ⓑ 1.5 inches
Ⓒ 2 inches
Ⓓ 2.2 inches

3. What is the median of the following set of numbers?
{16, −10, 13, −8, −1, 5, 7, 10}

Ⓐ −8
Ⓑ −1
Ⓒ 4
Ⓓ 6

4. Select the median number for each set of numbers.

	3	4	8
4, 2, 3, 6, 4, 9, 7	○	○	○
6, 3, 2, 8, 1, 3, 6	○	○	○
8, 9, 4, 8, 1, 10, 3	○	○	○

Correct Subject-Verb Agreement (L.6.1)

Day 2

5. Correct the following sentence to show subject-verb agreement.

Tracy and Gary likes to solve puzzles.

- Ⓐ Tracy and Gary likes to solve puzzles.
- Ⓑ Tracy and Gary like to solve puzzles.
- Ⓒ Tracy and Gary like to solves puzzle.
- Ⓓ Tracy likes to solve puzzle.

6. Correct the following sentence to show subject-verb agreement.

All of the students competes for the prizes.

- Ⓐ All of the student competes for the prizes.
- Ⓑ All of the students compete for the prizes.
- Ⓒ The students competes for the prizes.
- Ⓓ None of the above

7. Correct the following sentence to show subject-verb agreement.

Many people considers tea a stimulant.

- Ⓐ Many a people considers tea a stimulant.
- Ⓑ Many people consider tea a stimulant.
- Ⓒ Many peoples consider tea a stimulant.
- Ⓓ The above sentence needs no correction.

8. Correct the following sentence to show subject-verb agreement.

Tony climb the tree every day after school.

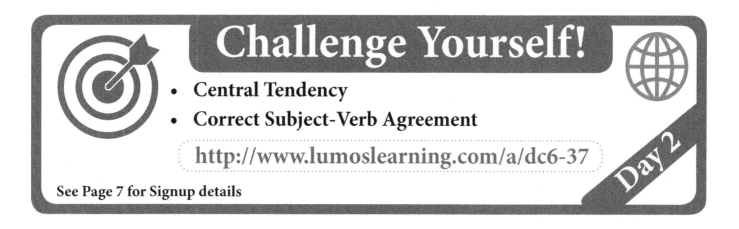

Challenge Yourself!

- Central Tendency
- Correct Subject-Verb Agreement

http://www.lumoslearning.com/a/dc6-37

Day 2

See Page 7 for Signup details

Graphs & Charts (6.SP.B.4)

Day 3

1. Which of the following graphs best represents the values in this table?

X	Y
1	1
2	3
3	1
4	3

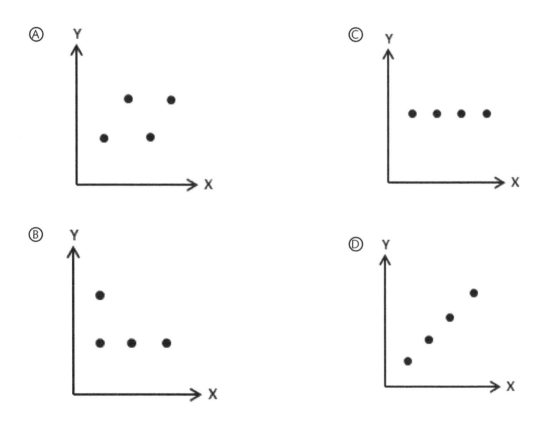

2. The results of the class' most recent science test are displayed in this histogram. Use the results to answer the question. A "passing" score is a 61 or higher.

   How many students passed the science test?

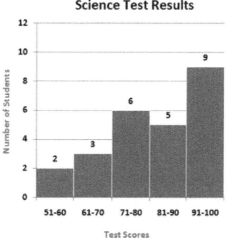

Science Test Results

   Ⓐ 3 students
   Ⓑ 20 students
   Ⓒ 23 students
   Ⓓ 25 students

3. The results of the class' most recent science test are displayed in this histogram. Use the results to answer the question. How many students scored a 90 or below?

   Ⓐ 5 students
   Ⓑ 9 students
   Ⓒ 11 students
   Ⓓ 16 students

Science Test Results

Refer below bar graph to answer the following questions.

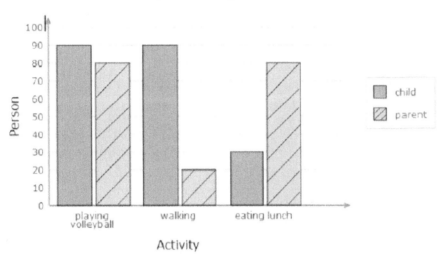

Family beach day

4. **Which of the following statements are true? Select all that apply.**

Ⓐ The same number of children participated in playing volleyball and walking
Ⓑ The same number of children participated in walking and eating lunch.
Ⓒ All of the children who played volleyball also ate lunch.
Ⓓ More children than parents ate lunch.
Ⓔ More children than parents played volleyball.
Ⓕ The same number of parents played volleyball as ate lunch.

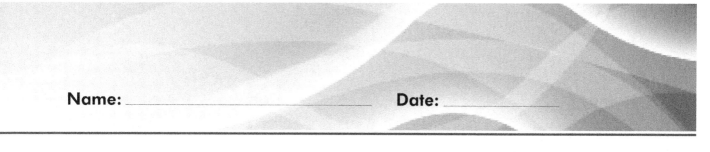

Demonstrate Command of Capitalization (L.6.2)

Day 3

5. Choose the answer with the correct placement of capital letters for the sentence below.

my doctor moved to phoenix, arizona.

- Ⓐ my doctor moved to phoenix, arizona.
- Ⓑ My doctor moved to Phoenix, Arizona.
- Ⓒ My doctor moved to phoenix, arizona.
- Ⓓ My doctor moved to phoenix, arizona.

6. Choose the answer with the correct placement of capital letters for the sentence below.

my mother called doctor billings to make an appointment for saturday.

- Ⓐ My mother called Doctor Billings to make an appointment for Saturday.
- Ⓑ my mother called doctor billings to make an appointment for Saturday.
- Ⓒ My mother called doctor billings to make an appointment for saturday.
- Ⓓ My mother called doctor Billings to make an appointment for Saturday.

7. Choose the answer with the correct placement of capital letters for the sentence below.

mother says he is the best doctor in santa maria.

- Ⓐ Mother says he is the best doctor in santa maria.
- Ⓑ Mother says he is the best doctor in Santa maria.
- Ⓒ Mother says he is the best doctor in Santa Maria.
- Ⓓ mother says he is the best Doctor in Santa maria.

8. Read the below sentence and rewrite it with correct placement of capital letters.

i live in malibu, california.

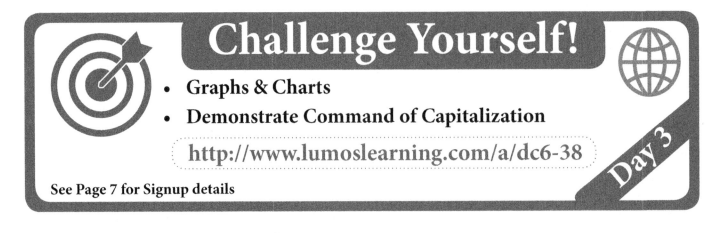

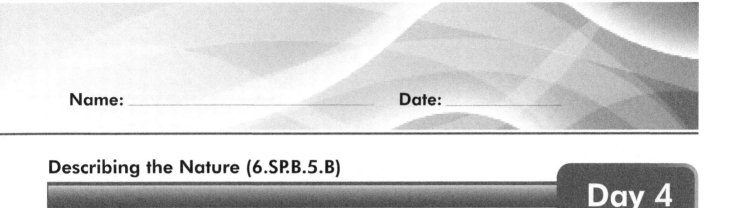
Describing the Nature (6.SP.B.5.B)

Day 4

1. A new sandwich shop just opened. It is offering a choice of ham sandwiches, chicken sandwiches, or hamburgers as the main course and French fries, potato salad, baked beans or coleslaw to go with them. How many different ways can a customer have a sandwich and one side order?

    Ⓐ 6
    Ⓑ 8
    Ⓒ 10
    Ⓓ 12

2. Karen has a set of numbers that she is working with. {6, 14, 28, 44, 2, −6} What will happen to the mean if she adds the number −8 to the set?

    Ⓐ The mean will decrease.
    Ⓑ The mean will increase.
    Ⓒ The mean will stay the same.
    Ⓓ It cannot be determined.

3. Susan goes to the store to buy supplies to make a cake. What is the average amount that Susan spent on each of the ingredients she bought?
    {$4.89, $2.13, $1.10, $3.75, $0.98, $2.46}

    Ⓐ $5.22
    Ⓑ $2.55
    Ⓒ $2.25
    Ⓓ $2.50

4. Dana's recent math exams grades were: 67, 62, 70, 69, 90, 93, 95, 88, and 93. What is Dana's median score? Circle the answer that represents the median score.

    Ⓐ 88
    Ⓑ 93
    Ⓒ 67

Analysis of Key Events and Ideas (RL.6.1)

Day 4

Once upon a time four boys lived in the countryside. One boy was very clever but he did not like books. His name was Good Sense. The other boys were not very clever but they read every book in the school. When they became grown men, they decided to go out into the world to earn their livelihood.

They left home and came to a forest where they halted for the night. When they woke up in the morning, they found the bones of a lion. Three of them, who had learned their books well at school, decided to make a lion out of the bones.

Good Sense told them, "A lion is a dangerous animal. It will kill us. Don't make a lion." But the three disregarded his advice and started making a lion. Good Sense was very clever. When his friends were busy making the lion, he climbed up a tree to save himself. No sooner had the three young men created the lion and gave it life, than it pounced upon them and ate them up. Good Sense climbed down the tree and went home very sadly.

5. What did they see in the forest when they woke up in the morning?

- Ⓐ the bones of a lion
- Ⓑ a witch that could bring an animal to life
- Ⓒ Good Sense hiding in a tree
- Ⓓ none of the above

6. What did the four friends decide when they became grown men?

- Ⓐ They decided to go out into the world and earn their livelihood.
- Ⓑ They decided to play with animal bones.
- Ⓒ They decided to be friends forever.
- Ⓓ They decided to never leave home.

7. What advice did Good Sense give his friends?

- Ⓐ He told them how to create the lion.
- Ⓑ He told them how to beat the lion once it was created.
- Ⓒ He told them not to create the lion.
- Ⓓ He told them to hide from the lion once they created it.

Faster than fairies, faster than witches,
Bridges and houses, hedges and ditches,
And charging along like troops in a battle,
All through the meadows the horses and cattle,
All of the sights of the hill and the plain,
Fly as thick as driving rain,
And ever again, in the wink of an eye,
Painted stations whistle by.

Here is a child who clambers and scrambles,
All by himself and gathering brambles;
Here is a tramp who stands and gazes,
And there is the green for stinging the daisies;
Here is a cart run away in the road,
Lumping along with man and load;
And here is a mill and there is a river,
Each a glimpse and gone forever.
-- R. L. STEVENSON

8. **What detail in the above poem tells us that this poem is about the view from inside a train?**

Ⓐ All of the sights of the hill and the plain, Fly as thick as driving rain
Ⓑ Faster than fairies, faster than witches, Bridges and houses, hedges and ditches,
Ⓒ And ever again, in the wink of an eye, Painted stations whistle by.
Ⓓ Here is a cart run away in the road

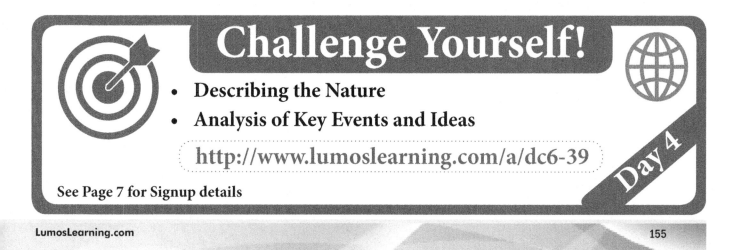

Challenge Yourself!

- **Describing the Nature**
- **Analysis of Key Events and Ideas**

http://www.lumoslearning.com/a/dc6-39

Day 4

See Page 7 for Signup details

Context of Data Gathered

Day 5

1. Bella recorded the number of newspapers left over at the end of each day for a week. What is the average number of newspapers left each day?

    3, 6, 1, 0, 2, 3, 6

    Ⓐ 2 newspapers
    Ⓑ 3 newspapers
    Ⓒ 4.3 newspapers
    Ⓓ 6 newspapers

2. Recorded below are the ages of eight friends. Which statement is true about this data set?

    13, 18, 14, 12, 15, 19, 11, 15

    Ⓐ Mean > Median > Mode
    Ⓑ Mode < Mean < Median
    Ⓒ Median > Mode < Median
    Ⓓ Mode > Mean > Median

3. The line plot below represents the high temperature in °F each day of a rafting trip. What was the average high temperature during the trip?

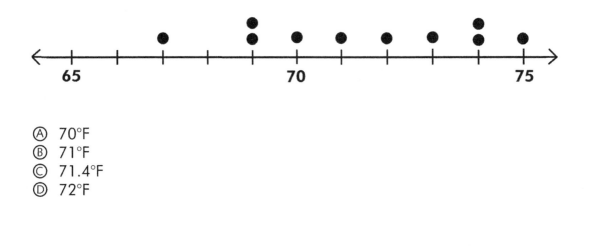

    Ⓐ 70°F
    Ⓑ 71°F
    Ⓒ 71.4°F
    Ⓓ 72°F

4. Frank played 9 basketball games this season. His scores were 15, 20, 14, 36, 20, 10, 35, 23, and 24. What is the median of Frank's scores? Write the answer in the box.

Conclusions Drawn from the Text (RL.6.1)

Day 5

Katie called out to her mother. The aroma of freshly brewed coffee filled the air. The sizzling sound of frying eggs reached her ears as she glided down the stairs. Now she could smell toast and bacon too. She ran to the table and sank into her seat just as her mother walked in from the kitchen. She was ready for _____

5. Complete the sentence above.

Ⓐ Dinner
Ⓑ Lunch
Ⓒ Breakfast
Ⓓ Sleeping

John wanted to buy some candy at the store. When he got there he realized he forgot his money.

6. What can you infer as the action that John could take that would have the most chance of succeeding?

Ⓐ John asked the store owner if he could pay him back another day.
Ⓑ John asked the store owner if he could work for the candy.
Ⓒ John walked outside and looked on the ground to see if anyone dropped money.
Ⓓ John walked back home and got the money he forgot.

It is recommended that people should exercise every day, particularly those who spend many hours doing sedentary activities like playing cards, reading, or playing video games.

7. We can infer that when people are doing sedentary activities, they must be _____.

Ⓐ Relaxing
Ⓑ Talking
Ⓒ Sitting
Ⓓ Jumping

Zoe is my dog, and she is white and brown. Zoe knows how to do a lot of tricks. Zoe can speak when you ask her to, and she can shake your hand. Zoe will also give you a kiss when you ask her. I don't know many dogs that can do these things.

8. What is the main idea of the passage? Circle the correct answer choice.

Ⓐ Zoe is my dog.
Ⓑ Zoe can give kisses.
Ⓒ Zoe is smart.
Ⓓ Zoe only knows a few tricks.

Challenge Yourself!

- **Context of Data Gathered**
- **Conclusions Drawn from the Text**

http://www.lumoslearning.com/a/dc6-40

Day 5

See Page 7 for Signup details

Name: _____   Date: _____

Online Review of Grade 7

Login to your student account and explore 7th Grade Math and English Language Arts topics!

Math	ELA
Ratios & Proportional Relationships The Number System Expressions & Equations Geometry Statistics & Probability	Reading Standards for Literature Reading Standards for Informational Text Language Standards Writing Standards

Hello Marisa Adams!

Try our new chrome extension - Lumos WordUp Vocabulary Practice ✖

Math

Expressions & Equations (1/5 Lessons) ●
40%

Geometry (1/6 Lessons) ●
40%

Ratios & Proportional Relationships (3/8 Lessons) ●
20%

Statistics & Probability (1/11 Lessons) ●
100%

The Number System (1/9 Lessons) ●
20%

ELA

Language Standards (1/18 Lessons) ●
20%

Reading Standards for Informational Text (1/9 Lessons) ●
40%

Reading Standards for Literature (1/12 Lessons) ●
40%

Writing Standards (1/13 Lessons) ●
50%

Your Study Programs:

7 MATH — Lumos StepUp - SBAC Online Practice and Assessments - Grade 7 Mathematics — 12% — 12%

7 ELA — Lumos StepUp - SBAC Online Practice and Assessments - Grade 7 ELA — 7%

This Week's Online Activities

- **Reading Assignment**
- **Vocabulary Practice**
- **Write Your Summer Diary**

http://www.lumoslearning.com/a/slh6-7

See Page 7 for Signup details

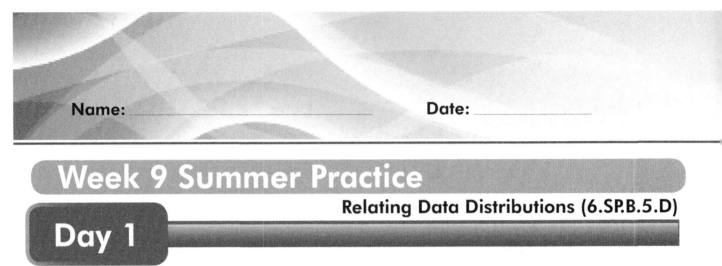

Week 9 Summer Practice

Relating Data Distributions (6.SP.B.5.D)

Day 1

1. The histogram below shows the grades in Mr. Didonato's history class.

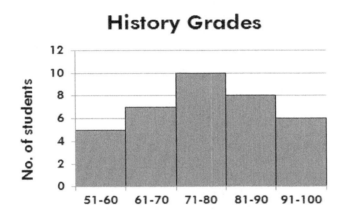

History Grades

Which of the following statements is true based on this data?

Ⓐ The mode score is 75%.
Ⓑ More than half the students received 81% or higher.
Ⓒ Ten students received a 70% or lower.
Ⓓ There is not enough information to determine the median score.

2. The bar graph below shows the different types of shoes sold by Active Feet.

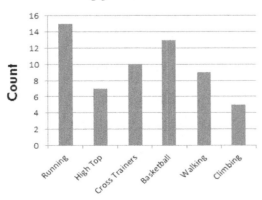

Types of Shoes

Which of the following statements is true based on this data?

Ⓐ The store carries more types of basketball and climbing shoes combined than types of running shoes.
Ⓑ The store sells more running shoes the any other shoe type.
Ⓒ The store has more types of walking shoes than cross trainers.
Ⓓ The store earns more money selling basketball shoes than walking shoes.

3. **Milo and Jacque went fishing and recorded the weight of their fish in the line plots below.**

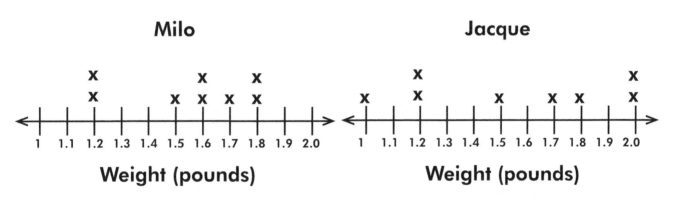

Milo   ## Jacque

Weight (pounds)   Weight (pounds)

Which of the following statements is true based on this data?

Ⓐ The weights of Milo's fish have more variability.
Ⓑ The average weight of Jacque's fish is greater than the average weight of Milo's fish.
Ⓒ The weights of Jacque's fish have a greater mean absolute deviation.
Ⓓ Milo caught more fish by weight than Jacque.

4. **Three volleyball teams each recorded their scores for their first 5 games. Use each team's scores below to determine the missing value.**

	10	14	17
Team 1: 15, 16, t, 17, 12, Mode = 17, What is t?	○	○	○
Team 2: 7, 14, r, 16, 13 Mean = 12, What is r?	○	○	○
Team 3: 11, 7, 19, 14, z, Median = 14, What is z?	○	○	○

Day 1

5. Choose the best possible supporting detail to most accurately complete the statements.

1. The beach is a perfect place to take a vacation.
2. I love to laze around on the sands.
3. _____
4. That is why I love to take a vacation at the beach.

   Ⓐ I love the smell of sea water.
   Ⓑ I hate the smell of sea water.
   Ⓒ Starfish are so cool.
   Ⓓ I like to see aircraft fly.

Allison went to swim practice and worked very hard to try and perfect her flip turn. A flip turn is a turn where you flip underwater and turn to go back in the direction that you came from. Allison practiced 1 hour before school and 3 hours after school each day. On the weekends she practiced 5 hours a day! Allison thought she would never get the flip turn down right, but she practiced and practiced. Finally, after two weeks straight of practicing, she nailed it.

6. Which statement indicates the primary message?

   Ⓐ If you practice less than two weeks, you won't accomplish your goal.
   Ⓑ Only practice on the weekends.
   Ⓒ Keep trying and don't give up.
   Ⓓ Keep trying, but give up if you get too tired.

Writing Task 1

7. **Writing Situation:** The park in your area has only one tennis court. It is always crowded and one has to wait at least two hours before getting a chance to play.

Writing Task: Write a persuasive letter to your mayor requesting more tennis courts in your area. In your letter, be sure to describe the situation and explain the reasons why you need more tennis courts.

8. Choose the best possible supporting detail to most accurately complete the statements.

1. Christmas is everybody's favorite holiday.
2. One gets to do a lot of shopping.
3. _____
4. That is why everybody loves Christmas.

Ⓐ   Christmas break is boring because you don't get to see your school friends every day.
Ⓑ   The school gives a lot of homework to do over the holidays.
Ⓒ   Decorating the Christmas tree is a lot of work.
Ⓓ   There's a spirit of giving.

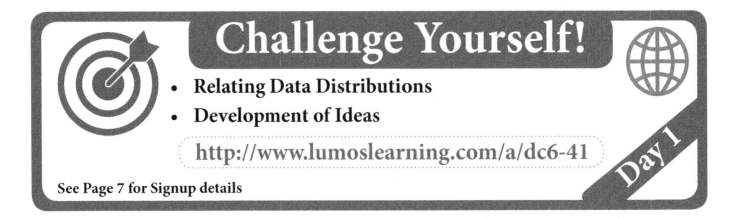

Challenge Yourself!
- **Relating Data Distributions**
- **Development of Ideas**

http://www.lumoslearning.com/a/dc6-41

Day 1

See Page 7 for Signup details

Data Interpretation (6.SP.B.5)

Day 2

1. In the last 4 seasons, Luis scored 14, 18, 15, and 25 goals. How many goals does he need to score this year, to end the season with an overall average of 20 goals per season?

   Ⓐ 29
   Ⓑ 27
   Ⓒ 30
   Ⓓ 28

2. Stacy has 60 pairs of shoes. She has shoes that have a heel height of between 1 inch and 4 inches. Stacy wants to know which heel height she has the most of. Would she figure out the mode or mean?

   Ⓐ Mean
   Ⓑ Mode
   Ⓒ Both
   Ⓓ Neither

3. There are three ice cream stands within 15 miles and they are owned by Mr. Sno.

Ice Cream Stand	Vanilla	Chocolate	Twist
A	15	22	10
B	24	8	14
C	20	16	13

   What percentage of the ice cream cones sold by Ice Cream Stand B were vanilla? Round your answer to the nearest whole number.

   Ⓐ 52%
   Ⓑ 24%
   Ⓒ 50%
   Ⓓ 25%

4. Scientists were concerned about the survival of the Mississippi Blue Catfish, so they collected data from samples of this species of fish. The scientists captured the fish, measured them, and then returned them to the lake from which they were taken. Select the correct numbers for different ranges of lengths.

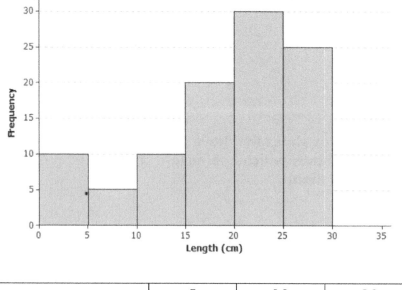

	5	10	20	25	30
0 – <5 cm	O	O	O	O	O
5 – <10 cm	O	O	O	O	O
10 – <15 cm	O	O	O	O	O
15 – <20 cm	O	O	O	O	O
20 – <25 cm	O	O	O	O	O

Summary of Text (RL.6.2)

Day 2

It is great to have a younger sibling. Some people may think it is annoying, but those people don't realize the benefits of having a younger sibling. First, a younger sibling can do your chores for you, so you don't get in trouble. Second, they can feed the animals, so you don't have to do that. Third, they can actually be fun to play with when you are stuck at home on a snow day.

5. What can you summarize from this passage?

Ⓐ It is great to have younger siblings.
Ⓑ Younger siblings are annoying.
Ⓒ You only want a sibling to be older than you.
Ⓓ Being an only child is the best.

Ryan earned money each week from doing chores around the house. His mother always told him that it was his money, but he should not spend it on useless things. Ryan decided to take $5.00 out of his piggy bank and went into the candy store. He looked at all the different types of candy and spent all of his $5.00.

6. What is the most important message in this passage?

Ⓐ Ryan loves candy.
Ⓑ Ryan begged for his money.
Ⓒ Ryan had a green piggy bank.
Ⓓ Ryan shared his candy with his friends.

The little girl got to pick out new furniture and decorate her room. She really liked the white bed and dresser. She decided to paint her walls pink and get a pink carpet. She was so excited to be getting a new room!

7. What can you summarize about this little girl?

Ⓐ She had always had a room to herself.
Ⓑ She was excited to redo her room the way she wanted.
Ⓒ She wanted to paint her room purple.
Ⓓ Her mother wasn't happy with her decisions.

I'm nobody! Who are you?

I'm nobody! Who are you?
Are you nobody, too?
Then there's a pair of us — don't tell!
They'd banish us; you know!

How dreary to be somebody!
How public like a frog
To tell one's name the livelong day
To an admiring bog!

-Emily Dickinson

Emily Dickinson is a well- known American poet who was born in the 1800's.

8. What do you think she is talking about in this poem?

- Ⓐ She feels as if people do not see or notice her, and she likes it that way.
- Ⓑ She wants to be a frog.
- Ⓒ She doesn't like being not noticed and does want to be important.
- Ⓓ She is not making any comparisons in this poem.

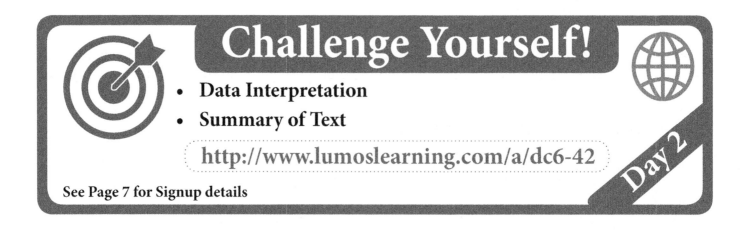

Challenge Yourself!

- **Data Interpretation**
- **Summary of Text**

http://www.lumoslearning.com/a/dc6-42

Day 2

See Page 7 for Signup details

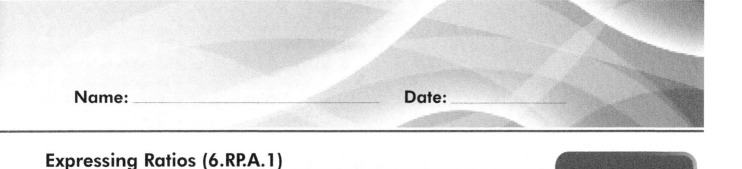

Expressing Ratios (6.RP.A.1)

Day 3

1. The little league team called the Hawks has 7 brunettes, 5 blonds, and 2 red heads. What is the ratio of redheads to the entire team in simplest terms?

   Ⓐ 2:7
   Ⓑ 2:5
   Ⓒ 2:12
   Ⓓ 1:7

2. The little league team called the Hawks has 7 brunettes, 5 blonds, and 2 red heads. The entire little league division that the Hawks belong to has the same ratio of redheads to everyone else. What is the total number of redheads in that division if the total number of players is 126?

   Ⓐ 9
   Ⓑ 14
   Ⓒ 18
   Ⓓ 24

3. Barnaby decided to count the number of ducks and geese flying south for the winter. The first day he counted 175 ducks and 63 geese. What is the ratio of ducks to the total number of birds flying overhead in simplest terms?

   Ⓐ 175:63
   Ⓑ 175:238
   Ⓒ 25:9
   Ⓓ 25:34

4. Complete the following table by filling in the blanks with a number that shows the correct ratio that is equivalent to the one shown in the first row.

1	2
2	4
	6
4	8
5	
	12

Use Clues To Determine Multiple-meaning Words (L.6.4)

Day 3

Crab and shrimp: they're not just for dinner anymore. A natural polymer found in the exoskeletons of crustaceans can keep your car cleaner. Never heard of chitosan? You may not be able to say that for long. Researchers in the School of Fashion and Textiles at RMIT are using the biopolymer, found in the exoskeletons of crustaceans such as crabs and shrimp, to coat the 100% polyester fabric used in automobiles. Combining fragrant oils with the polymer, which has the ability to form an antimicrobial film, creates a durable, fragrant finish in the fabric.

5. Based on this passage, crabs and shrimp are _____.

- Ⓐ dinner
- Ⓑ fragrant
- Ⓒ crustaceans
- Ⓓ polyester

A natural polymer found in the exoskeletons of crustaceans can keep your car cleaner. Researchers in the School of Fashion and Textiles at RMIT are using the biopolymer, found in the exoskeletons of crustaceans such as crabs and shrimp, to coat the 100% polyester fabric used in automobiles. Combining fragrance oils with the polymer, which has the ability to form an antimicrobial film, creates a durable, fragrant finish in the fabric.

6. Based on the prefix "exo-," and prior knowledge about crabs and shrimp, an exoskeleton is probably: _____.

- Ⓐ a skeleton that is outside the body
- Ⓑ a skeleton that is inside the body
- Ⓒ a soft skeleton
- Ⓓ a durable skeleton

Researchers at RMIT's School of Fashion and Textiles are developing anti-stain, antimicrobial, and anti-odor textiles that keep car interiors clean and sweet-smelling.

7. Anti-odor and sweet-smelling textiles are _____.

- Ⓐ stainless
- Ⓑ fragrant
- Ⓒ durable
- Ⓓ smelly

8. Choose the answer that contains opposites.

- Ⓐ Blunt, sharp
- Ⓑ Careful, caring
- Ⓒ Cold, cool
- Ⓓ Dirty, gross

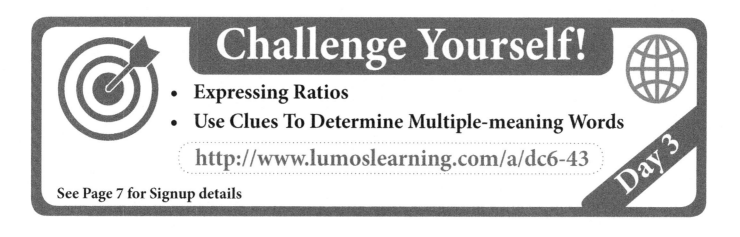

Challenge Yourself!

- **Expressing Ratios**
- **Use Clues To Determine Multiple-meaning Words**

http://www.lumoslearning.com/a/dc6-43

Day 3

See Page 7 for Signup details

Unit Rates (6.RP.A.2)

Day 4

1. Don has two jobs. For Job 1, he earns $7.55 an hour. For Job 2, he earns $8.45 an hour. Last week he worked at the first job for 10 hours and at the second job for 15 hours. What were his average earnings per hour?

    Ⓐ $8.00
    Ⓑ $8.09
    Ⓒ $8.15
    Ⓓ $8.13

2. It took Marjorie 15 minutes to drive from her house to her daughter's school. If the school was 4 miles away from her house, what was her unit rate of speed?

    Ⓐ 16 mph
    Ⓑ 8 mph
    Ⓒ 4 mph
    Ⓓ 30 mph

3. The Belmont race track known as "Big Sandy" is 1½ miles long. In 1973, Secretariat won the Belmont Stakes race in 2 minutes and 30 seconds. Assuming he ran on "Big Sandy", what was his unit speed?

    Ⓐ 30 mph
    Ⓑ 40 mph
    Ⓒ 36 mph
    Ⓓ 38 mph

4. Check the box in each row that represents the correct unit rate for each situation.

	1:10	1:5	1:50	1:20
$1.00 per 5 pounds	○	○	○	○
50 pounds per box	○	○	○	○
10 miles per gallon	○	○	○	○
1 lap in 20 minutes	○	○	○	○

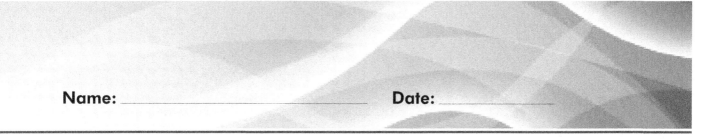

Characters Responses and Changes (RL.6.3)

Day 4

The sky was dark and overcast. It had been raining all night long and there was no sign of it stopping. I thought that my Sunday would be ruined. As it poured outside, I settled down by the window to watch the rain. The park opposite my house looked even more green and fresh than usual. The branches of the tall trees swayed so hard in the strong wind that I thought they would break. A few children were splashing about in the mud puddles and having a wonderful time. I wished I could join them too! There were very few people out on the road and those who were hurried on their way, wrapped in raincoats and carrying umbrellas.

My mother announced that lunch was ready. It was piping hot and very welcoming in the damp weather. We spent the afternoon listening to music and to the downpour outside.

In the evening we chatted and made paper boats that we meant to sail in the stream of water outside. It was not a bad day after all!

5. Who is the main character in the above passage?

    Ⓐ The rain
    Ⓑ The writer's mom
    Ⓒ The writer
    Ⓓ The wind

6. The character in a story who dominates is a _____.

    Ⓐ minor character
    Ⓑ major character
    Ⓒ supporting character
    Ⓓ Joker

Having to start at a new school didn't worry Jane at all; she was ready for anything.

7. A character trait of Jane is _____.

    Ⓐ Easy-going
    Ⓑ Shy
    Ⓒ Scared
    Ⓓ Nervous

Ever since Greg was little, he always liked to take things apart. He took apart his sister's dolls, took apart all his trucks and cars, and even took apart his parents' telephone to see how it worked.

8. A character trait of Greg is_____?

Ⓐ Destructive
Ⓑ Angry
Ⓒ Curious
Ⓓ Mean

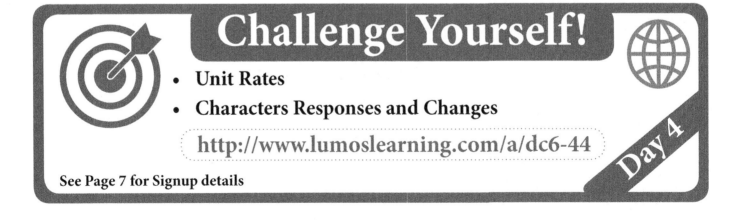

Challenge Yourself!

- Unit Rates
- Characters Responses and Changes

http://www.lumoslearning.com/a/dc6-44

Day 4

See Page 7 for Signup details

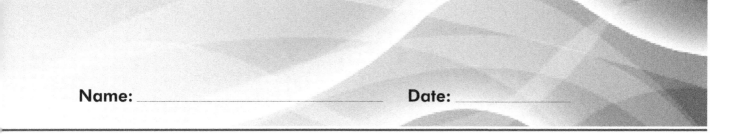
Day 5

Solving Real World Ratio Problems (6.RP.A.3)

1. **Michael Jordan is six feet 6 inches tall. How much is that in inches?**

   Ⓐ 66 inches
   Ⓑ 76 inches
   Ⓒ 86 inches
   Ⓓ 78 inches

2. **What is 7.5% in decimal notation?**

   Ⓐ 0.75
   Ⓑ 0.075
   Ⓒ 0.0075
   Ⓓ 7.5

3. **A $60 shirt is on sale for 30% off. How much is the shirt's sale price?**

   Ⓐ $30
   Ⓑ $40
   Ⓒ $18
   Ⓓ $42

4. **To make yummy fruit punch, use 2 cups of grape juice for every 3 cups of apple juice. Select all of the juice combinations below that correctly follow this recipe ratio.**

   Ⓐ 4 cups grape juice: 6 cups apple juice
   Ⓑ 5 cups grape juice: 10 cups apple juice
   Ⓒ 6 cups grape juice: 9 cups apple juice
   Ⓓ 6 cups grape juice: 12 cups apple juice
   Ⓔ All of the above

Figurative Words and Phrases (RL.6.4)

Day 5

5. Choose the word below that is closest in meaning to the figurative expression.

He works like a _____.

- Ⓐ Lion
- Ⓑ Dog
- Ⓒ Parrot
- Ⓓ Cat

6. Choose the word below that is closest in meaning to the figurative expression.

He is as stubborn as a _____.

- Ⓐ mule
- Ⓑ cow
- Ⓒ baby
- Ⓓ ice

7. Choose the sentence below that is closest in meaning to the figurative expression.

The secretary had a mountain of paper work. _____.

- Ⓐ The secretary was dealing with paper art
- Ⓑ The secretary had a large amount of work
- Ⓒ The secretary had to run around a lot
- Ⓓ The secretary had to meet a lot of people

8. Choose the sentence below that is closest in meaning to the figurative expression.

He quit smoking cold turkey.

Ⓐ He quit eating poultry.
Ⓑ He quit cooking.
Ⓒ He quit smoking suddenly and without help.
Ⓓ He quit smoking Turkish cigars.

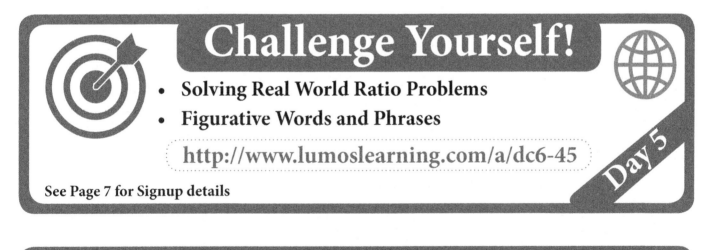

Challenge Yourself!

- **Solving Real World Ratio Problems**
- **Figurative Words and Phrases**

http://www.lumoslearning.com/a/dc6-45

Day 5

See Page 7 for Signup details

This Week's Online Activities

- **Reading Assignment**
- **Vocabulary Practice**
- **Write Your Summer Diary**

http://www.lumoslearning.com/a/slh6-7

See Page 7 for Signup details

Week 10

Lumos Short Story Competition 2021

Write a short story based on your summer experiences and get a chance to win $100 cash prize + 1 year free subscription to Lumos StepUp + trophy with a certificate.
To enter the competition follow the instructions.

Step 1

Visit **www.lumoslearning.com/a/tedbooks**
and enter your access code to create Lumos parent and student account.
Access Code : G6-7MLSLH-73094

Step 2

After registration, your child can upload their summer story by logging into the student portal and clicking on **Lumos Short Story Competition 2021.**

Note: Please do not register again, If you have already registered this book and are using online resources. Students can simply log in to the student portal and submit their story for the competition. Visit: www.lumoslearning.com/a/slh2021 for more information

Last date for submission is August 31, 2021
Use the space provided below for scratch work before uploading your summer story.
Scratch Work

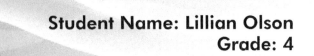

2020 Winning Story

Finding Fun during a Pandemic

This was a weird summer. We did not travel because of COVID-19 and stayed mostly at home and outside around our house. Even when I saw my friends, it was unusual. This summer, I worked and made money helping my parents.

The pandemic allowed me to spend more time inside and I learned many new skills. We made face masks and had to figure out which pattern fits us the best. My sister and I enjoyed creating other arts and crafts projects. Additionally, I have been learning to play instruments such as the piano, guitar, and trombone. We also baked and cooked because we did not go out to eat (at all!). I love baking desserts. The brownies and cookies we made were amazing! I also read for one hour a day and did a workbook by Lumos Learning. I especially loved Math.

Our time outdoors was different this summer. We ordered hens. My family spent a lot of time fixing the coop and setting it up for our 18 chickens. We had a daily responsibility to take care of our chickens in the morning, giving them food and water and in the evening, securing them in their coop. We were surprised that 3 of the hens were actually roosters! Additionally, we exhausted many days gardening and building a retaining wall. Our garden has many different fruits and vegetables. The retaining wall required many heavy bricks, shoveling rocks, and moving dirt around. To cool off from doing all this hard work, we jumped in a stream and went tubing. Our dog, Coco liked to join us.

COVID-19 has also caused me to interact differently with my friends. We used FaceTime, Zoom, and Messenger Kids to chat and video talk with each other. Video chatting is not as fun as being in person with my friends. I love Messenger Kids because it is fun and you can play interactive games with each other.

I had to spend some of my time working. I helped clean my parents' Airbnb. This was busier because of COVID-19. My sister and I will start to sell the chicken eggs once they start to lay which we expect to happen anytime. We had a small business two years ago doing this same thing.

Summer 2020 has been unusual in many ways. We played indoors and outdoors at our house and nearby with family. I have learned new skills and learned to use technology in different ways. Summer of 2020 will never be forgotten!

Submit Your Story Online & WIN Prizes!!!

2019 Winning Story

I used to spend my summer playing video games. I spent my summer in other unproductive ways. That's the way I spent my summer until my dad bought me a Lumos Learning book. To be honest, I didn't really want to use my Lumos Learning book, but I did and I loved using it. What I really liked about it was the laugh practices. My favorite laugh practice is on page 20. It reminded me of everything I learned in the school year.

The Lumos learning book wasn't the only fun thing about my summer, my family also went to Canada! We were supposed to go to Canada on an airplane but our flight got canceled, so we had to go on a 9-hour road trip. Canada was a cool place. My family and I had lots of fun. We only went to Canada because one of Dad's colleagues was getting married. When we went to eat in a giant paper/plastic tent the yellow rice had too much sugar but the meat and the spices tasted really good. The bugs, flies, and mosquitos were big, but not very big compared to the size of a human. After we finished eating, we left.

On the wedding day, I was very confused about why we were all had to wear turbans, why some people had swords, why we were sitting on the floor, and what the people were saying and why there was a tomb with an old man sitting in front of it in the Sikh temple. After that, I was very interested in Indian culture.

A few days after that, when we returned home to New York, I went to the YMCA summer camp. We stayed in the Gymnasium singing camp songs and after that, my group's counselor paired us up with partners, and before long everyone had a partner. 2 We also went to Highland Park and we played a game where there is a president and a bodyguard and a circle of people around the president and bodyguard and the people try to use a ball to hit the president (The President and the bodyguard can shift positions and the bodyguard has to stand in front of the president).

After that, we went back inside and did some research on Dr. Seuss. Then, we went to eat lunch outside, but there were a lot of bugs outside. After that we played lots and lots of games until it was pickup time. Even though my summer was a little rough, I had a great time and by the time the next school year starts, I'll be ready for fourth grade.

Submit Your Story Online & WIN Prizes!!!

Answer Key &
Detailed Explanations

Question No.	Answer	Detailed Explanations
1	C	First, to find the proper ratio, subtract the number of girls from the total number of students. The difference is the number of boys. $600-330 = 270$. So, the initial ratio is $\frac{270}{600}$. Then, to rewrite a ratio in its simplest terms, divide the numerator and denominator by the Greatest Common Factor (GCF). Here, the GCF is 30. 270 divided by 30 = 9 and 600 divided by 30 = 20, so, the simplest ratio is $\frac{9}{20}$.
2	D	First, find the ratio of emeralds to rubies. That ratio is $\frac{85}{119}$. To find how many pearls the sultan had, set up a proportion with the ratio of diamonds to pearls: $\frac{85}{119} = 45/x$ Then, find the cross products of each: $85*x = 119*45$ Simplify: $85x = 5355$ Solve for x by dividing by 85 on both sides: $\frac{85x}{85} = \frac{5355}{85}$ $x = 63$
3	B	$75 + 125 = 200$. Therefore, the total number of birds is 200. The ratio of geese to total birds is 75:200. Simplify the ratio by dividing by the GCF (75,200)= 25, simplified ratio is 3:8.
4	4:5	4:5. There are 4 white stars and 5 gray stars.
5	B	The author used very descriptive language to pull the reader in. The author wants the reader to be able to imagine what the moment is like. It was raining and the wind was blowing, but the author's point was for the reader to be able to picture it.
6	B	Although the author is talking about the night owl, the point of view is actually that of the author
7	A	The poem mentions that it's a night bird and, at the end, again mentions night. The answer is A.
8	Ring	Ring. This is given in the very first paragraph of the passage

Question No.	Answer	Detailed Explanations
1	C	$\frac{1}{5}$ = a unit price of $0.20 per piece $\frac{.85}{4}$ = a unit price of $0.2125 per piece $\frac{.25}{2}$ = a unit price of $0.125 per piece. This is the best price per unit. $\frac{1.1}{6}$ = a unit price of $0.183 per piece.
2	C	The unit rate at Store A is $\frac{\$3.45}{5}$=$0.69. 20 cans of beans would be $0.69*20= $13.80 The unit rate at Store C is $\frac{\$2.46}{4}$= $0.615. 20 cans of beans would be $0.615*20=$12.30. Subtract $13.80−12.30=$1.50
3	B	284 miles divided by 58 miles per hour are how you will find how long it took Beverly to make the trip. (Distance ÷ rate = time) $\frac{284}{58} \approx$ 4.9 hours 0.9 hours = 54 minutes (Multiply 60 by 0.9, because there are 60 minutes in an hour.) 4 hours and 54 minutes is how long it took Beverly to make the trip.
4	$ 0.40	The bag shown in the picture consists of 8 apples. To determine the unit rate for the cost of one apple, divide the cost of all the apples by the total number of apples: $3.20 ÷ 8 = .40 So, one apple has a unit rate cost of $.40.
5	A	The correct answer is A. Sarah's mother told her that it was going to rain, but Sarah chose to ignore her mother's advice. None of the other answers are true. There is no evidence that she doesn't love her mother, and if she didn't like getting wet then she would have definitely listened to her mother. She did not obey her mother, so answer choice D is not correct.
6	C	The correct answer is C. Sarah would not have argued about whether or not to take an umbrella if it were raining. She would not need an umbrella if it were snowing or if it were warm.

Question No.	Answer	Detailed Explanations
7	B	The correct answer is B. We can tell that it is a negative emotion that the boy is feeling - so that eliminates A and D. If he were scared, he would likely want to be WITH people, not away from them.
8	Fall	Pumpkins are associated with fall and Halloween, and that is the only season where the leaves change color.

Question No.	Answer	Detailed Explanation
1	D	1000 grams/1 kilogram = 375 grams/x kilograms 1000x = 375 Divide each side by 1000 x = 0.375 kilograms
2	D	36 inches equal 1 yard, so 72 inches must equal 2 yards.
3	B	is/of = %/100 so: x/120 = 50/100 100*x = 120*50 100x = 6000 Divide both sides by 100 x = 60

4

Feet	Yards
3	1
6	2
9	3
15	5
24	8

1 yard = 3 feet
Set up the proportion: yard/feet
(1) Let x be the number of yards in 6 feet.

$$\frac{1}{3} = \frac{x}{6}$$

$3x = 1 \times 6 = 6$

$x = \frac{6}{3} = 2$ yards

(2) Let y be the number of feet in 3 yards

$$\frac{1}{3} = \frac{3}{y}$$

$1 \times y = 3 \times 3 = 9$ or $y = 9$

(3) Let z be the number of yards in 24 feet.

$$\frac{1}{3} = \frac{z}{24}$$

$3z = 1 \times 24 = 24$

$z = \frac{24}{3} = 8$

Question No.	Answer	Detailed Explanations
5	D	The correct answer is D because it is a good ending sentence and sums up the point of the paragraph. A and B are too specific, and C is repetitive.
6	A	The only answer that is a concluding sentence is answer choice A. It mentions class president, which is the point of the article. The other three answers are specific details and do not sum up the passage.
7	D	Answer choice D is correct. It correctly summarizes the point of the article. The other three answers do not make sense if you read the passage carefully.
8	preservative	preservative. This is given in the very first paragraph of the passage.

Question No.	Answer	Detailed Explanation
1	C	Find the unit rate for one juice pouch. $$\frac{\$6.00}{12} = \frac{x}{1}$$ 6*1=12*x 6 = 12x Divide both sides by 12 x = $0.50 per pouch
2	B	Find the unit rate for one gallon of gas. 128/4 = x/1 128*1=4*x 128 = 4x Divide both sides by 4 x = 32 miles per gallon
3	D	Find the unit rate for one mile. 39/6 = x/1 39*1=6*x 39 = 6x Divide both sides by 6 x = 6.5 or 6 minutes 30 seconds
4	5	Since 3 cheeseburgers cost $15, when you divide $15 by 3, you get cost of one cheeseburger, which is $5.
5	B	Answer choice B is correct because the story specifically says that the policeman asked the writer for his name and address. You assume that the man gave it to him.
6		By reading this you can conclude that Thomas likes sports. Based on the fact that Thomas plays so many sports and likes to run in his free time, we can conclude that he likes sports.
7	D	Because he is being so careful, you know that ladders can be dangerous. The correct answer is D. Age is never mentioned, neither is ladders being easy or fun.
8	A	The correct answer is A. The paragraph mentions nothing about students who enjoy math and it doesn't mention how many to buy. It also does not say anything about not needing all of the items.

Question No.	Answer	Detailed Explanations

1   **B**

is/of = %/100

$$\frac{x}{24} = \frac{25}{100}$$

x*100 = 24*25

100x = 600

Divide both sides by 100

x = 6

2   **A**

is/of = %/100

$$\frac{x}{60} = \frac{15}{100}$$

x*100 = 60*15

100x = 900

Divide both sides by 100

x = 9

3   **C**

is/of = %/100

$$\frac{9}{72} = \frac{x}{100}$$

9*100 = 72*x

900 = 72x

Divide both sides by 72

x = 12.5%

4

Item Purchased	Original Price	Amount of Discount	Amount Paid
Video Game	$80	20%	**$64**
Movie Ticket	$14	**20%**	$11.20
Laptop	$1,000	**25%**	$750
Shoes	$55.00	10%	$49.5

Amount paid for video game = $64, Because $80 x 0.80 = $64 (20% discount means, one has to pay 80% of the original price. 80% = 0.80)

(2) Original price of the movie ticket = $14

Amount paid = $ 11.2

Discount = 14 - 11.2 = 2.8

% Discount /100 = Discount / original price

% Discount = 100 x (Discount / original price) = 100 x $(\frac{2.8}{14}) = \frac{280}{14}$

= 20%

Question No.	Answer	Detailed Explanations
4 Contd...		(3) Discount for the Laptop = 1000 - 750 = 250 % Discount = 100 x (Discount / original price) = 100 x ($\frac{250}{1000}$) = $\frac{25000}{1000}$ = 25%
5	D	Answer choice D is correct. There are only three characters in the story; the writer, the writer's friend, and the policeman. Although the actor is mentioned, he is not an actual character.
6	C	The correct answer is C. They were talking about the man in the musical show they had just seen.
7	D	The answer choice is D. Risking his own life to save a dog's life shows the man thinks of others more than himself.
8		The answer should include that the magician wanted Aladdin to give him the lamp, but Aladdin could not at the time.

Day 1

Question No.	Answer	Detailed Explanation
1	B	There are 12 inches in a foot. 69 inches * (1 foot/12 inches) = 69/12 = 5.75 feet
2	D	There are 4 quarts to a gallon. 7*4 = 28 quarts 28 + 3 = 31 quarts
3	D	There are 100 cm in a meter and 1000 meters in a kilometer. 3.7 km * (1000 m/1 km) * (100 cm/1 m) = 370,000 cm

4				
1	3 L	**3000 ml**	Because 3 x 1000 =3000
2	**5 g**	5000 mg	Because 5000 ÷ 1000 = 5
3	**8 m**	8000 mm	Because 8000 ÷ 1000 = 8
4	12 L	**12,000 ml**	Because 12 x 1000 =12,000
5	20 g	**20,000 mg**	Because 20 x 1000=20,000

Question No.	Answer	Detailed Explanation
5	A	The answer is A. "dead to the world" means that he was asleep. He would not stay at home if he was not breathing or unconscious; he would be removed immediately and his family would be upset.
6	A	Being in hot water means being in trouble, so answer choice A is correct.
7	A	The correct answer is A. There is no such thing as a circular file, so the only possibility is the trashcan. To say that means to throw something away.
8	A	Bugging someone and bothering someone are the same thing, so the correct answer is A.

Week 2

Day 2

Question No.	Answer	Detailed Explanation

1   A

The original problem is:

$$\frac{20}{1} \div \frac{1}{4} =$$

To divide fractions, you must Keep (the first fraction), Change (the division to multiplication), and Flip (the second fraction, or, take the reciprocal).

$$\frac{20}{1} \times \frac{4}{1} = \frac{80}{1} = 80$$

2   D

The original problem is:

$$1\frac{1}{2} \div \frac{3}{4} =$$

First, find the improper fraction of the first mixed number (numerator = bottom times the side plus the top) = [(2*1)+1], Fraction = $\frac{3}{2}$

To divide fractions, you must keep (the first fraction), Change (the division to multiplication), Flip (the second fraction, or, take the reciprocal).

$$\frac{3}{2} \times \frac{4}{3} = \frac{12}{6}$$

Simplify by factoring out the GCF of 6.
The answer is $\frac{2}{1}$ or 2

Question No.	Answer	Detailed Explanation
3	D	The original problem is: $3\frac{2}{3} \div 2\frac{1}{6} =$ First, find the improper fraction of the first mixed number (numerator = bottom times the side plus the top) = [(3*3)+2], Fraction=$\frac{11}{3}$. Then, find the improper fraction of the second mixed number (numerator = bottom times the side plus the top = [(2*6)+1], Fraction = $\frac{13}{6}$ To divide fractions, you must keep (the first fraction), Change (the division to multiplication), Flip (the second fraction, or, take the reciprocal). $\frac{11}{3} \times \frac{6}{13} = \frac{66}{39}$ Simplify by factoring out the GCF of 3. The answer is $\frac{22}{13}$ Divide $\frac{22}{13}$ to get a mixed number: The answer is $1\frac{9}{13}$
4	$\frac{1}{8}$	$\frac{1}{8}$. Because $\frac{1}{2} \div \frac{4}{1} = \frac{1}{2} \times \frac{1}{4} = \frac{1}{8}$
5	A	Thrifty means that you don't want to spend money unless you have to and you want to save as much as possible. Answer choice A is correct.
6	B	Because the author of this sentence admitted that he/she didn't like the trait, we know there is a negative spin on the part of the author. That's why the correct answer is B.
7	C	'Courageous' is the word with the positive connotation.
8	B	The girl obviously has no respect for anyone or anything. She would be classified a brat for sure. B is the correct answer.

Question No.	Answer	Detailed Explanation
1	A	First, find the difference of $1,800 − $315 = $1,485 Then, divide $1,485/11 = $135
2	D	To find the answer, divide $3,960 ÷ 55. (Note: The $125 is unnecessary information.)
3	C	1 hour = 60 minutes, so 2 hours = 120 minutes So, 9,000 ÷ 120 = 75
4	1575	We have to find the number, which when multiplied with 26 gives 40,950. Number x 26 = 40,950. Or Number = 40,950 divided by 26. Use the standard long division algorithm to get the answer: 1,575
5	B	Answer choice B is correct. Based on the sentences, it is clear that the person being discussed has come to fame recently.
6	A	The first part of the poem is how the owl comes out of the tree into the forest at night. The correct answer is A.
7	D	The poet said all of the above things in the opening lines of the poem.
8	A	Answer choice A shows us the lesson in the passage.

Day 4

Question No.	Answer	Detailed Explanation
1	A	$7.25 + $8.16 + $5.44 = $20.85 $20.85/3 = $6.95
2	D	The standard form would be written as 20.063 since the whole number part is 20 and the decimal part is written .063 (Sixty-three thousandths).
3	B	$160 + $12.50 = $172.50 (His total investment) $215.00 − $172.50 = $42.50
4	22.72	Answer is 22.72 Because 71 x 32 = 2272. The factors have a total of 2 decimal places, therefore the answer should have 2 decimal places: 22.72
5	A	Based on the details in the passage, it is obvious that the writer is a child still living at home. They discuss doing things that would take place in a home. For those reasons, the correct answer is A.
6	C	The story specifically says that it took place long after people had gone to bed, so answer choice C is correct.
7	C	The correct answer is C. The story specifically says that the robbery was going to take place during dinner time and it was going to be at the green and gold bank
8	D	All of the things mentioned are in Washington, D.C., our nation's capital.

Question No.	Answer	Detailed Explanation
1	D	All statements are true. A number is always a factor and a multiple of itself. It is prime because the only two factors are 1 and 17.
2	A	Other than 1, which is not prime by definition, 2, 3, 5, and 7 are the only single-digit numbers that can be divided by only themselves and 1.
3	C	A prime number is a whole number (greater than 1) which is divisible by only 1 and itself. The set {7, 23, 47} contains three numbers which fit the definition stated above. Each number is divisible by only 1 and itself.
4	12	The Common Factors of 24, 36 and 48 are: 24: 1, 2, 3, 4, 6, 8, **12**, 24 36: 1, 2, 3, 4, 6, 9, **12**, 18, 36 48: 1, 2, 3, 4, 6, 8, **12**, 16, 24, 48 Hence, the Greatest Common Factor (GCF) is **12**.
5		Based on what he says, you can tell that these words are from the wolf's perspective.
6	A	In the above passage the wolf claims that allergies were to blame and he didn't want to hurt the pigs. That is very different from the traditional story.
7	B	He is trying to act innocent by saying he never meant to hurt the pigs.
8	C	Because "I" is used, we know that it is written from first person point of view.

Day 1

Question No.	Answer	Detailed Explanation
1	D	Larissa has 4 1/2 cups of flour. Amount of flour needed to make cookies = 2 3/4 cups of flour. Amount of flour left after making cookies = 4 1/2 - 2 3/4 4 1/2 - 2 3/4 = 9/2 - 11/4 = (9x2)/(2x2) - 11/4 = 18/4 - 11/4 = (18-11)/4 = 7/4 = 1 3/4
2	D	$2,123 − 2,400 = −$277 They must make a deposit of $277 in order to prevent the account from being overdrawn.
3	B	1 + 4 − 2 = 3
4	57	Answer is 57, because from 0 to 30 is a difference of 30 steps; 0 to -27 is a difference of 27 steps. Combined, this is a difference of 57 steps on the number line.
5	B	They are both talking about what types of leadership are best. They weren't just talking about inspiration and influence, but they were talking about leadership by inspiration and influence. Answer choice B is correct.
6	C	Based on the passage, we know that in both figures all of the angles are 90 degree angles (right angles). The correct answer is C.
7		Based on the passage, we know that a square is defined as having all sides equal whereas the opposite sides of a rectangle are parallel and congruent.
8	B	Answer choice B is the most similar because you use soap and water and have to rinse and dry them.

Question No.	Answer	Detailed Explanation
1	D	−4 is only 4 units away from 0 on a number line. All of the other numbers are farther away.
2	A	If you count the units between −5.5 and 7.5, you will count 13 units between them.
3	D	

The number line above shows −1, 3, and 4.
All other answer choices are not represented on this number line. |
4	A, C, & D	3 is a positive number, therefore it is greater than 0. All negative numbers are less than 0.
5	A	The text specifically states that an empty gallery had 42,000 germs but when filled with people, that same gallery had nearly 5,000,000 germs. One can then conclude that a crowded space will hold more germs. The correct answer is A.
6	D	While Louis Pasteur discovered germs there is no evidence in the story to support that he liked counting germs. Yes, germs are too small to be seen with the naked eye but they can be seen using powerful microscopes. Even though people do carry germs, the best concluding statement from this passage would be that there are fewer germs in fresh air. The correct answer is D.
7	B	While Michael Jordan did star in a movie with Bugs Bunny, this is not the most significant part of the passage. Yes, it tells a little about Michael Jordan's life but it is not his life story, it is mere- ly highlights of his career as a famous basketball player. Since the passage tells primarily about Michael Jordan as a basketball player and all he has accomplished, it can be concluded that the author wrote the passage to show what a great basketball player he is. The correct answer is B.
8	D	It says in the text that the nervous system tells the body what to do. It other words, it controls the body.

Question No.	Answer	Detailed Explanation
1	B	Quadrant II – In this quadrant the x-coordinate is negative and the y-coordinate is positive.
2	D	Quadrant IV – In this quadrant the x-coordinate is positive and the y-coordinate is negative.
3	C	Quadrant III – In this quadrant both the x-coordinate and y-coordinate are negative.
4	(6,4)	(6,4) because the plotted point is 6 lines on the horizontally x-axis and four lines vertically on the y-axis.
5	B	The main idea is that mountain men liked Shakespeare, even if they could not read. Sentence six exemplifies this idea the most.
6	D	More men had Shakespeare than the Bible, and they memorized Shakespeare. That shows how much they loved it.
7	A	The fact that mountain men carried books around for years does not directly prove that they liked Shakespeare best.
8		The entire area is about washing clothes

Question No.	Answer	Detailed Explanation
1	C	Distance between 9 and 16 = 7. Distance between two consecutive ticks = 7/7 = 1. Therefore the red dot represents the number 14.
2	C	Distance between -5 and 3 = 8. Distance between two consecutive ticks = 8/8 = 1. Therefore the red dot represents the number 0.
3	C	Distance between -2 and 14 = 16. Distance between two consecutive ticks = 16/8 = 2. Therefore the red dot represents the number 4.
4	B & C	Negative numbers are smaller than zero. Positive numbers are greater than zero. (B) and(C) are correct.
5	B	Answer choices A, C, and D present minor details related to the bigger, overall topic that germs are everywhere. The correct answer is B.
6	C	Answer choice C is the only answer that is not even presented in the story; therefore it is not a supporting detail. The correct answer is C.
7	A	While each of the answer choices are true, only answer choice A illustrates how books were important to mountain men and that was because they were hard to get.
8	B	The author specifically states that certain parts of clothing or dress need special attention or care. The author then goes on to support this idea. The correct answer choice is B.

Question No.	Answer	Detailed Explanation
1	B	$17 - |(7)(-3)|$ $= 17 - |-21|$ $= 17 - 21$ $= -4$ Note: Absolute value (the value of $|x|$) is the value of a number without regard to its sign.
2	A	$16 + |(7)(-3) - 44| - 5$ $= 16 + |-21 - 44| - 5$ $= 16 + |- 21 + (-44)| - 5$ $= 16 + |-65| - 5$ $= 16 + 65 - 5$ $= 81 - 5$ $= 76$ Note: Absolute value (the value of $|x|$) is the value of a number without regard to its sign.
3	A	$|15 - 47| + 9 - |(-2)(-4) - 17|$ $= |-32| + 9 - |8 - 17|$ $= 32 + 9 - |-9|$ $= 32 + 9 - 9$ $= 41-9$ $= 32$ Note: Absolute value (the value of $|x|$) is the value of a number without regard to its sign.
4	- 14	$|14| - |-28|$ $= 14 - 28 = -14$
5	A	Answer A is correct because synonyms will basically have the same definition as the original word they are representing.
6	D	The words will have completely opposite meanings, so the answer is D.

Question No.	Answer	Detailed Explanation
7	C	<u>homophone</u> - same pronunciation, spelled differently, different meanings. <u>homonyms</u> - same spelling, different meaning. <u>homographs</u> - spelled the same, not necessarily pronounced the same, and different meaning <u>homo-word</u> - not found in grammar, <u>minute</u> - time is pronounced with a short vowel i and the u sounds like a short vowel i. <u>minute</u> - small is pronounced with a long vowel i and a long vowel u. Hence, answer choice C is correct. These are homographs.
8	D	Answer choice D is correct because those two words are complete opposites.

Question No.	Answer	Detailed Explanation
1	A	-7 is greater than -12 so Xavier has the higher score.
2	A	Get a common denominator and compare fractions. The LCM between 6 and 12 is 12. Kelly: $\frac{(5 \times 2)}{(6 \times 2)} = \frac{10}{12}$ Helen: $\frac{9}{12}$ Kelly has read more because $\frac{10}{12} > \frac{9}{12}$ or $\frac{5}{6} > \frac{9}{12}$.
3	D	$-52°F > -80°F$ $-52°F$ is 52 degrees below zero whereas $-80°F$ is 80 degrees below zero.
4	56	The answer is 56 degrees. Comparing the 2 values, 32 or 56, 56 degrees would be more hotter when compared to 32 degrees.
5	B	If you chose B, the missing sentence should be second, you made the best choice. Although it says "Start," you cannot start until you know what you are starting to do, so the missing sentence should not be first. You should select the freshest bread before you take the pieces of it, so the missing sentence should not be third, and it would not make sense in the fourth position.
6	C	If you chose C, the missing sentence should be third, you picked the right answer. The phrase, "continue the aerobic training" lets you know that aerobic training had to have already begun at some point, and it is mentioned in the second sentence.
7	D	The salutation is the beginning of the letter where you say "Dear Sir or Madam".
8	C	Although there will be description of some kind, there will be more in the narrative and the descriptive writing about a winter day will have the most.

Question No.	Answer	Detailed Explanation
1	C	The absolute value of a number is its distance from zero on a number line. Distance between two consecutive ticks on the number line is 1 unit. So the number represented by the dot is 3. The $\lvert 3 \rvert$ is 3 because it is three units from 0.
2	C	The absolute value of a number is its distance from zero on a number line. Distance between two consecutive ticks on the number line is 0.5 units. So the number represented by the dot is -1. The $\lvert -1 \rvert$ is 1 because it is 1 unit from 0.
3	A	The absolute value of a number is its distance from zero on a number line. $\lvert -27 \rvert = 27$ and $27 > 19$. Therefore $\lvert -27 \rvert > 19$.
4		-5, -1, 2 because negative numbers fall the left of the 0.
5	C	The passage is trying to persuade the reader as to why dogs are better pets than cats. The correct answer is C.
6	A	The passage is giving information on how words are added to or deleted from the dictionary. The correct answer is A.
7	A	The passage ends by saying "you should eat vegetables at least 3 meals a day." It also gives information to backup why this is important. Therefore, the passage is trying to convince readers to eat more vegetables. The correct answer is A.
8	B	While Michael Jordan did star in a movie with Bugs Bunny, this is not the most significant part of the passage. Yes, it tells a little about Michael Jordan's life but it is not his life story, it is merely highlights of his career as a famous basketball player. Since the passage tells primarily about Michael Jordan as a basketball player and all he has accomplished, it can be concluded that the author wrote the passage to show what a great basketball player he is. The correct answer is B.

Day 3

Question No.	Answer	Detailed Explanation
1	B	A negative account balance indicates a debt is owed. $-\$45$ means $45 is owed. $-\$5$ means $5 is owed. Therefore the account balance of $-\$45$ represents the greatest debt.
2	A	The warmer temperatures are above zero. Of these two $5°F >$ $2°F$. Therefore the warmest temperature is $5°F$ above zero.
3	A	First calculate the amount Anneliese spent: $\$58.00 + \$35.00 =$ $\$93.00$. If her account balance is $-\$142.00$ then before she spent any money she had $-\$142.00 + \$93.00 = -\$49.00$.
4	1	Answer is 1, because the absolute value of 12 is 12, and of -11 is 11. So 12 - 11 = 1.
5	C	All of the evidence in the passage points to the fact that Jordan was a truly great basketball player. That is why the main idea can be found in answer choice C.
6	D	It was not mentioned in the passage that he was the best player on the team. The only detail that supports the main idea is D, he contributed to many of the Bulls' wins.
7	B	The claim, or controlling idea, is usually at the beginning of the paragraph. That is true in this case. The answer is B because that's what the first sentence says.
8		The opening sentence is the claim, or the controlling idea i.e., Smartphones are the newest innovative technology out there.

Day 4

Question No.	Answer	Detailed Explanation
1	B	Move on the x axis from −3.6, four units to the right to 0.4 (East is to the right on this map.) Then move on the y axis from −2.6, six units up to 3.4 (North is up on this map.) So, the coordinates are (0.4, 3.4).
2	D	In Quadrant II, the x value is negative and the y value is positive. The coordinates would be (−5, 8).
3	B	Absolute value is the positive value of a number. That makes the ordered pair (4, 4).
4	B, D & E	

Coordinates mentioned in options (B), (D) and (E) would fall in Quadrant I (Q I) because, points in Q I have positive x - coordinates and positive y - coordinates.

Question No.	Answer	Detailed Explanation
5	B	Both men are talking about how peace can only be attained through non-violence and understanding. The correct answer is B.
6	C	Both quotations, while having a different message, speak about the importance and value of music. The correct answer choice is C.

Question No.	Answer	Detailed Explanation
7	D	You can use all of the above to effectively compare and contrast.
8	Polar regions	Polar regions are the only logical answer because they are cold and icy.

Question No.	Answer	Detailed Explanation
1	B	The base is 5. The exponent is 3. 5 is multiplied 3 times, or 5 X 5 X 5 = 125
2	C	The base is 2. Count the factors. There are 6. 6 is the exponent. $2 * 2 * 2 * 2 * 2 * 2 = 2^6$
3	D	The base is y. Count the factors. There are 4. 4 is the exponent. $y * y * y * y = y^4$
4	4096	8 x 8 x 8 x 8 = 4,096
5	A	The answer is A, colorful. Adjectives are words that describe nouns, and colorful describes the pages. Reading is a verb (with the helping verb was.) Pages and book are both nouns because they are things.
6	B	The answer is B. Adjectives are words that describe nouns, and beautiful describes the noun planet. Earth is a proper noun and both system and plant are nouns.
7	C	The correct answer is C. Alien and airship are both nouns and ran is a verb. Frightened is the only describing word.
8	hardly	Adverbs answer the questions **how, how often, when, where, how much, or to what extent**. "hardly" This tells us **to what extent** the printer works.

Day 1

Question No.	Answer	Detailed Explanation
1	A	Since 3(n + 7) is equal to 33, then (n + 7) must equal 11 (3 x 11 = 33). Therefore, n must equal 4, since 4 + 7 = 11.
2	B	A number joined to a variable through multiplication is a coefficient. 22 is the coefficient of x.
3	A	When n = 7, the expression becomes 5(7 - 5) = 5 (2) = 10.
4	B & C	B and C, The order of the numbers should match the phrase.
5	B	Answer choice B is correct. "Myself" is a reflexive pronoun. None of the other answer choices sound correct.
6	B	The correct answer is B, "ourselves", because "we" is the subject. That tells us that it is more than one person and the author is included in the decorating.
7	B	Because "she" is used in the sentence, we know the answer is B "herself". The other three answers do not make sense in the sentence.
8	Walking and running are fun, too.	You have to say "walking and running" again. Otherwise, it is not clear if they are talking about "walking and running" or "team sports".

Question No.	Answer	Detailed Explanation
1	C	$(4 - 2) \rightarrow$ The difference of 4 and 2. $6(4 - 2) \rightarrow$ The product of 6 and the difference of 4 and 2.
2	B	$(8 \div 2) \rightarrow$ The quotient of 8 and 2. $- 10 \rightarrow$ less 10 or 10 subtracted from. $(8 \div 2) - 10 \rightarrow$ 10 less than the quotient of 8 and 2.
3	D	A coefficient is the number mutiplied by a variable. In this expression there are two variable terms, 2x and 9x. The coefficients are 2 and 9.
4	A & B	A. (2+1) + (2+1) + (2+1) B. 6 + 3
5		Since each student is singular, his/her will be the correct answer.
6		While we know that her is a pronoun for girl, it is still not the correct answer choice because the sentence references girls (plural) and her is a singular pronoun. Their is the correct word.
7		Since we know that Coach Bob is a boy and is singular, the correct answer would be "his."
8	A	The only answer choice that is grammatically correct is A, I. "Billy and me," does not sound right, nor does "Billy and us" or "Billy and his."

Question No.	Answer	Detailed Explanation	
1	A	$y = 3x - 13$	Original equation
		$y = 3(6) - 13$	Substitute 6 for x
		$y = 18 - 13$	Multiply
		$y = 5$	Subtract
2	B	$y = \frac{1}{4}x \div 2$	Original equation
		$y = \frac{1}{4}(32) \div 2$	Substitute 32 for x
		$y = \frac{32}{4} \div 2$	Multiply
		$y = 8 \div 2$	Simplify fraction
		$y = 4$	Divide
3	D	$3a^2 - 7b$	Original equation
		$3(3)^2 - 7(-8)$	Substitute 3 for a and −8 for b
		$3(9) - 7(-8)$	Exponents
		$27 - 7(-8)$	Multiply
		$27 - (-56)$	Multiply
		$27 + 56$	Change to adding
		83	Add
4	B, C, & D	B. $56 - 7 = 49$	
		C. $3(7) + 4 = 25$	
		D. $7 \times 7 \times 7 = 343$	
5	A	The antecedent in the sentence is anybody, which is singular, therefore the correct pronoun would be his. The correct answer is A.	
6	B	The antecedent in the sentence is students, which is plural, therefore the correct pronoun would be their. No other pronoun makes sense. The correct answer is B	
7	D	The antecedent in the sentence is Gavin, which is a single boy, therefore the correct pronoun would be him. The correct answer is D.	
8	she	The antecedent in the sentence is Patty. Since Patty is a singular girl, the correct pronoun is she.	

Week 5

Day 4

Question No.	Answer	Detailed Explanation
1	D	The expression, $3(n - 4)$, is equivalent because it has the same value as the original. The GCF (Greatest Common Factor) of 3 has been factored out from each term.
2	B	Here, the variable is the common factor and can be factored out $n(2 - 7)$. Then, simplify within the parentheses: $n(-5)$. Finally, use the Commutative Property to rewrite the expression, coefficient first: $-5n$.
3	B	$5y + 2z - 3y + z = 2y + 3z$ Combine the like terms to simplify: $5y + 2z - 3y + z = (5y - 3y) + (2z + z) = 2y + 3z$.
4	(4 x 5) -3	(4 x 5) -3
5	D	The sentence says that mom made cookies yesterday which means it happened in the past. Therefore, you need to find an answer that is written in the past tense. Answer choice B is future. Answer choices A, C, and D are all past but only D makes sense. The correct answer is D.
6	A	The word "went" tells us this sentence is written in past tense. The only answer that is in past tense and makes sense is A, "bought."
7	B	While they're sounds right, the correct word would actually be their as it shows possession. They're represents 'they are' and that would not make sense in the sentence. The correct answer is B.
8	happily	The correct adverb to complete the sentence is "happily."

Question No.	Answer	Detailed Explanation
1	B	$(\frac{5}{25})$x and $(\frac{1}{5})$x are equivalent because $\frac{5}{25}$ simplifies to $\frac{1}{5}$. The expressions will be equivalent even if a number is substituted for x.
2	C	$7 + 21v$ and $7(1 + 3v)$ are equivalent because if you distribute 7 to $1 + 3v$ you will get $7 + 21v$. The expressions will be equivalent even if a number is substituted for v.
3	C	32p/2 and 16p are equivalent because if you divide 32p by 2 you get 16p. The expressions will be equivalent even if a number is substituted for p.
4	12 y	$8y + 8y + 8y = 24y$. Therefore given expression $= 24y/2 = (24/2)y = 12y$.
5	A	You must have quotations around what is said out loud. For that reason, answer choice A is correct.
6	C	Answer choice C is correct. There are two comma rules in place here. There needs to be a comma in items in a series (bananas, oranges, and cherries) and there is a compound sentence, so there needs to be a comma before the but.
7	A	Answer choice A is correct. There needs to be a semicolon after year because there are two complete sentences. You can't just put them together with a comma. It has to be a comma and a conjunction or a semicolon.
8		Michelle made pizza, grilled cheese, and tacos for lunch, but she didn't realize it was only 10:00 a.m.

Week 6

Day 1

Question No.	Answer	Detailed Explanation
1	B	x can be any whole number from 1 to 20, inclusive of 20.
2	A	"17 is less than or equal to" means $17 \leq$ "the product of 6 and q" means to multiply 6 and q, or 6q $17 \leq 6q$
3	C	"The quotient of d and 5" means to divide d by 5 "is 15" means "equals 15". $\frac{d}{5} = 15$
4	A, B & C	1, 2, and 4 would complete the equation with a value < 15.
5	B	Answer choice B is correct because that is the correct spelling of the flour that you cook with. This type of flour is made from grinding wheat.
6	C	Answer choice C is the correct word for the type of flowers mentioned in the sentence. The other options do not make sense in the sentence.
7	B	Answer choice B is correct. Stair is the correct spelling as the word is used in the sentence. Option A is a homophone. Option C is another word for guiding.
8	itinerary	It is a a planned route or journey.

Question No.	Answer	Detailed Explanation
1	B	Half of 117 can be expressed as (1/2)(117). x less than that is expressed as − x. (1/2)(117) − x.
2	B	Start with $20.00. Then add what he earned mowing the lawn (+c). Then subtract what he spent at the candy store (−x). The expression is $20 + c − x.
3	B	Clinton made a total of 23 items, so you know the expression has to equal 23. He made 6 dessert and 12 appetizers. You do not know how many main courses he made, so that is represented by x. 6 + 12 + x = 23
4	B & E	x > 5 and 5 < x
5	D	The sentences can be combined to make a compound sentence using the conjunction so. The correct answer is D.
6	A	The sentences can be combined to make a compound sentence using the conjunction but. The correct answer is A.
7	A	The sentence fragment, after school, can be used as a dependent clause to make a complex sentence. The correct answer is A.
8	B	Using the adjective brown to describe the puppy and listing its other attributes creates the best sentence. The correct answer is B.

Question No.	Answer	Detailed Explanation
1	D	Each time a number from x is multiplied by 8, the product is found in y. So, the equation is $y = 8x$.
2	D	To find the value of x, you must isolate it. Divide each side by -7. $-7x/-7 = 56/-7$. $x = -8$
3	B	Each value of y is the square of the corresponding x value. This is not a linear relationship.
4	A & C	A. $3(6 + k) = 42$ $\quad (3 \times 6) + (3 \times 8) = 42$ $\quad 18 + 24 = 42$ C. $8k - 4 = 60$ $\quad 8(8) - 4 = 60$ $\quad 64 - 4 = 60$
5	A	While each sentence says basically the same thing, only the first sentence paints the clearest picture of what was actually happening. The correct answer is A.
6	B	While each sentence has the same meaning, sentence B uses the most descriptive words and style.
7	D	Each sentence adds just a little more detail to better explain the topic. Answer choice D is correct.
8	B	While Beth thought the test was challenging, Mary thought it was easy.

Question No.	Answer	Detailed Explanation
1	A	Half of 12 is 6. Less than 6 caterpillars turned into butterflies. That means that x < 6.
2	D	Elliot has at least 5 different favorite foods. That means that he has more than 5 favorite foods. He could have an infinite number of favorite foods because there is no constraint on the number of favorite foods he could have.
3	D	There can be no more than 549 red crayons because that is the maximum number of crayons in the box. You know there are at least 8 red crayons, which means that x is greater than or equal to 8 and less than or equal to 549. $8 \leq x \leq 549$
4	E	Closed circle represents "Greater than or equal to" or "less than or equal to" on the number line. An arrow to the left represents "less than". $x \leq -15$
5	B	Julio was happy, not disappointed, but the text tells us that he was also something else. Satisfied and pleased are very similar to happy, so they are not something else. He expected other boys to win the title, so the best use of context to figure out the word "astounded" is to select "very surprised."
6	C	The signal word "but" tells us that the opposite of flimsy is strong because spider silk is stronger than steel.
7	C	Because it was summer, we know that sweltering means hot. It would never be cold on a beach in the summer.
8	Ugly	We know that it will be a word with a negative connotation and the only negative word that fits the sentence .

Week 6

Day 5

Question No.	Answer	Detailed Explanation
1	B	"m" represents the amount of money that Logan needs. "p" represents the number of pounds that Logan buys. The amount of money Logan needs is found by multiplying the cost of the candy by the number of pounds that Logan buys. m = 0.79(p)
2	B	m = $0.84(3) m = $2.52
3	A	"t" represents the total amount Norman spent. "g" represents the number of gallons that Norman purchased. To find the total amount that Norman spent, multiply the price of the gas by the total number of gallons that Norman purchased. t = g(3.55)

Question 4:

Day	Money Spent on Sodas	Sodas Purchased	Price per Soda
Monday	$30.00	24	$1.25
Wednesday	$57.50	46	$1.25
Friday	$41.25	33	$1.25

m = $30.00
24 x $1.25 = $30
w = 46 sodas
$57.50 / $1.25 = 46
f = 33 sodas
$41.25/ $1.25 = 33

Question No.	Answer	Detailed Explanation
5	D	An affix can either be a prefix or a suffix, but a suffix will never be at the beginning of a word. Suffixes are only at the ends of words. The correct answer is D.
6	A	Incapable and not being able to do something are the same thing, so the only possible answer is A.
7	C	"-age" is the suffix that is the same in all three words. The correct answer is C.
8	yield	yield or surrender is the exact definition of cede.

Question No.	Answer	Detailed Explanation
1	B	Area of a rectangle = length x width. A = 9 x 7 A = 63
2	D	Area of a square = (length of side)^2. A = 6^2 A = 36
3	D	Area of a parallelogram = base x height. A= 7 x 3 A = 21
4	78 km^2	Area = ½ (base x height) b = 12 km h = 13 km So, ½ (12 x 13) = area ½ (156) = 78 km^2
5	B	Alphabetize means to rearrange the words in the order that they would appear in the dictionary. Answer choice B is the only one where the words are correctly alphabetized.
6	D	Alphabetize means to rearrange the words in the order that they would appear in the dictionary. Answer choice D is the only one where the words are alphabetized correctly.
7	D	Alphabetize means to rearrange the words in the order that they would appear in the dictionary. Answer choice D is the only one where the words are alphabetized correctly.
8	3 Syllables	Organized is 3 syllables.

Question No.	Answer	Detailed Explanation
1	B	A prism has rectangular faces connecting the two bases. A trapezoid has four sides, so four rectangular faces are on a trapezoidal prism.
2	D	A rhombus is a parallelogram that is a quadrilateral and is equilateral.
3	C	Since the volume of a cube is found using the formula: V = (side length)^3, the length of each side of this cube would be 10 [V = (10)(10)(10)]. The surface area of a cube is found by finding the area of one face: A = (side)^2, then multiplying by 6, since there are 6 faces, so 6(side)^2. $6(10)^2 = 6(10)(10) = 6(100) = 600$
4	$27\frac{3}{5}$ cm^3	$V = lwh$ cm^3 = $(4\frac{3}{5})$ (3) (2) $V = (\frac{23}{5})$ (3) (2) $V = \frac{23 \times 3 \times 2}{5} = \frac{138}{5} = 27\frac{3}{5}$ cm^3
5	B	Based upon the usage in the sentence, the word "misplaced" means to lose. The correct answer is B.
6	C	While the word "brisk" can mean both fast and cool, in this particular sentence it means "cool." The correct answer is C.
7	C	Since Natalie and Sophia are looking forward to their ride, the answer must have a positive connotation. The correct answer is "exciting," C.
8	A	"Ravenous" means to be hungry. The correct answer is A. The context clues in the sentences help you determine this.

Question No.	Answer	Detailed Explanation
1	A	When the points are connected, Angles A and E are right angles and Angles B, C, and D are all obtuse angles.
2	D	When the points are correctly connected, a trapezoid is created.
3	A	A 180 degree clockwise rotation about the origin will cause the top of the triangle to point to the bottom, and also the shape to shift from Quadrant I to Quadrant III.
4	72 square units	72 square units. 6 units along the x-axis multiplied by 12 units along the y-axis equals. 72 total square units.
5	D	The sentence uses the repeated sound /j/ so it is an example of alliteration and a comparison using "like" so it is also an example of a simile.
6	A	The sentence does not mean to literally not spill the beans but rather not tell a secret. The correct answer is A, idiom.
7	B	The sentence is comparing a sandwich to a car using "as" which means it is a simile.
8		"Stop pulling my leg" does not mean that someone is literally pulling one's leg. It means to stop teasing. This is an idiom.

Week 7

Question No.	Answer	Detailed Explanation
1	A	When the exposed edges are connected a rectangular prism will be formed.
2	A	When the exposed edges are connected a cube will be formed.
3	C	When the exposed edges are connected a triangular prism will be formed.
4	76 square units	To find the surface area, find the area of each side using the net S.A. = (5*4) + (5*4) + (4*2) + (4*2) + (5*2) + (5*2) = = 20 + 20 + 8 + 8 + 10 + 10 = 76 square units
5	A	The reason the flights were cancelled was the blizzard, so answer choice A is the only one that is correct.
6	B	The flood is what caused the people to be left homeless, so answer choice B is correct.
7	C	Pedro got the job because of his friendly attitude, so answer choice C is correct.
8		**Cause** - Whistling at work and **Effect** - Task becomes easier

Question No.	Answer	Detailed Explanation
1	B	Add the number of boys who participated in each activity to find the total number of boys. 19 + 20 + 17 + 12 = 68
2	C	When conducting a survey, it is most accurate to ask the question to the focus group you are trying to reach.
3	D	Taking the temperature consistently at the warmest and coolest time of the day will provide a consistent data sample for Emily's survey.
4	B, C, D & E	Options (B), (C), (D), and (E) are correct, A statistical question is one that can be answered by collecting data that vary (i.e., not all of the data values are the same).
5	B	"Denotation" is the dictionary or literal meaning of a word. The correct answer is B.
6	C	"Connotation" refers to how the word makes us feel. The correct answer is C.
7	D	All the words listed have the same denotation as the word "house."
8	C	A nice, or positive, way to say old is to say that someone is "elderly."

Question No.	Answer	Detailed Explanation
1	B	The Socks section has a measure of 30 degrees and the Pants section has a measure of 145 degrees. Solve for the total pant sales by setting up a proportion and solving. 145/30 = x/$60 (145)($60) = 30x 8700 = 30x 290 = x Therefore, 300 is the best estimate.
2	C	The graph shows that there are 19 boys and 11 girls participating in the Jazz Band. 19 + 11 = 30 sixth graders altogether
3	A	Angle corresponding to R + B songs = 90 degrees. The number of R + B songs downloaded is 400 x (90/360) = 400 x (1/4) = 100 songs (90/360 = 1/4 after taking GCF 90 out of both the numerator and denominator) Angle correspoding to rock songs is close to 90 degrees but less than 90 degrees. Let us take it to be 75 degrees (approximately) So, number of rock songs downloaded is 400 x (75/360) = 400 x (5/24) = 83 (approximately) (75/360 = 5/24 after taking GCF 15 out of both the numerator and denominator) Therefore A.J. has downloaded 100 - 83 = 17 more R + B songs than rock songs. Among the choices given, (A) is the most appropriate choice.
4		City A = 33.75m City B = 22.50 m City C = 29 m Find the sum of the height of all four buildings and divide by 4 to determine the mean.
5	B	Answer choice B is an example of the word racket when it means noise.

Question No.	Answer	Detailed Explanation
6	D	In answer choice D, since the person has to bear weight or hold themselves up on their broken ankle, it is the correct answer.
7	C	If the little boy is being patient in line then he is quietly waiting. The correct answer is C.
8	D	The best thing a team could be would be diligent about practicing. The correct answer choice is D.

Question No.	Answer	Detailed Explanation
1	B	To find the average (mean) height of the plants, the heights would first be totaled. Then the total would be divided by 9 (the number of plants in all). $12 + 15 + 11 + 17 + 19 + 21 + 13 + 11 + 16 = 135$. 135 divided by 9 equals 15. The average (mean) height is 15 centimeters. To find the median height, the numbers would be arranged in increasing order. The ordered set becomes: {11, 11, 12, 13, 15, 16, 17, 19, 21} The median is the middle value: 15 centimeters.
2	D	To find the average heel height, first figure out how many of each height Stacy has. Create an equation to figure out the number of 4 inch heels that Stacy has. Add $20 + 15 + 20 + x = 60$ $55 + x = 60$ $x = 5$ Set up an equation to figure out the mean. You need to multiply the number of shoes and the heel height and then add them together and divide by the number of shoes. $$\frac{1(20) + 2(15) + 3(20) + 4(5)}{60} = x$$ $x = 2.2$ inches

Question No.	Answer	Detailed Explanation
3	D	To find the median, rearrange the numbers in the data set from lowest to highest. {16, −10, 13, −8, −1, 5, 7, 10} −10, −8, −1, 5, 7, 10, 13, 16 Because this set has an even number of terms, add the two middle numbers together and divide by 2. 5 + 7 = 12 12/2 = 6 6 is the median.

4

	3	4	8
4, 2, 3, 6, 4, 9, 7		●	
6, 3, 2, 8, 1, 3, 6	●		
8, 9, 4, 8, 1, 10, 3			●

To determine the median number, first, order the set of numbers from least to greatest. The median number will be the number in the center.

Question No.	Answer	Detailed Explanation
5	B	The suject is plural (Tracy and Gary), so there needs to be a plural subject (one with no "s" on the end.)
6	B	"All" is a plural subject, so you need a plural verb (one without an "s".)
7	B	The subject of the sentence is people, which is plural. That means the verb needs to be plural (which means that the verb does not have an "s".)
8	Tony climbs the tree every day after school.	Tony is one person (singular subject), so it needs a singular verb (one with an "s".)

Question No.	Answer	Detailed Explanation
1	A	Using the data to create ordered pairs (x, y), the first choice is the only graph that accurately represents the ordered pairs.
2	C	To find the number of students who passed, add the number of students who scored in the ranges of 61 – 70 (3), 71 – 80 (6), 81–90 (5), and 91 –100 (9). 3 + 6 + 5 + 9 = 23 students
3	D	To find the number of students who scored a 90 or below, add the number of students who scored in the ranges of 51 – 60 (2), 61 – 70 (3), 71 – 80 (6), 81–90 (5). 2 + 3 + 6 + 5 = 16 students
4	A, E, & F	A. 90 children participated in volleyball and 90 children participated in walking. E. 90 children played volleyball and only 80 parents played volleyball. F. 80 parents played volleyball and 80 parents ate lunch.
5	B	Answer choice B is correct. The beginning of the sentence should be capitalized. Also the city and state should be capitalized.
6	A	The correct answer is A. "My should be capitalized because it's the beginning of the sentence. "Doctor Billings" should be capitalized because that's his name. Saturday should be capitalized because it's one of the days of the week.
7	C	Answer choice C is correct. "Mother" should be capitalized because it is the beginning of the sentence. "Santa Maria" should be capitalized because it's a proper noun, the name of a place. "Doctor" should not be capitalized because it's not the name of a specific doctor.
8	I live in Malibu, California.	Malibu and California should be capitalized because they are proper nouns.

Day 4

Question No.	Answer	Detailed Explanation
1	D	Use the counting principle to determine the number of combinations if there are 3 types of sandwiches and 4 types of sides for lunch by: 3 * 4 = 12 There are 12 options.
2	A	{6, 14, 28, 44, 2, −6} the mean is 14.6 {6, 14, 28, 44, 2, −6, −8} the mean is 11.4 The mean will decrease with the addition of the number −8.
3	B	To find the average, add all of the prices together and divide by the number of ingredients, which is 6. $$\frac{\$4.89 + \$2.13 + \$1.10 + \$3.75 + \$0.98 + \$2.46}{6} = \$2.55$$
4	A	Dana's median score is 88.
5	A	Answer A is correct. Upon reading the passage, you will see in the second paragraph that it directly says that they found the bones of a lion.
6	A	If you chose A, you read the passage correctly. The last sentence in the first paragraph gives the correct answer.
7	C	If you chose answer C, you got it right. Good Sense told the other men NOT to create the lion.
8	C	Answer choice C is correct. The fact that it goes by stations tells you that you're on a train.

Week 8

Day 5

Question No.	Answer	Detailed Explanation
1	B	Find the total number of newspapers leftover and divide by the number of days. $\frac{3+6+1+0+2+3+6}{7} = \frac{21}{7} = 3$ newspapers
2	D	Find the mean, median, and mode of the data set and compare. Mean: $\frac{13+18+14+12+15+19+11+15}{8} = \frac{117}{8} = 14.625$ Median: 11, 12, 13, 14, 15, 15, 18, 19 → 14.5 Mode: 15 Mode > Mean > Median
3	C	Add the temperatures and divide by the number of temperatures. $\frac{67+69+69+70+71+72+73+74+74+75}{10} = \frac{714}{10} = 71.4°F$
4	20	To find the median score, order the numbers from least to greatest. 10, 14, 15, 20, 20, 23, 24, 35, 36 Then identify the number that is in the middle. In this list, 20 is in the middle of the list so the median is 20.
5	C	The correct answer is C. All of the foods mentioned were breakfast foods, so you can assume that breakfast is being cooked. Also, coffee is usually brewed first thing in the morning.
6	D	In this day and age, it is not likely that the store owner would let him pay him later or work off the candy. John would have to go home and get the money and walk back to the store.
7	C	The correct answer is C. If the article is saying that these people need to be active, then we can assume that they normally do a lot of sitting.
8	C	The author is proud of his/her dog and is saying that the dog can learn tricks and therefore, the dog is really smart.

Day 1

Question No.	Answer	Detailed Explanation

1   **D**

False. There is not enough information to determine the mode score.

False. There are 14 out of 36 students who received an 81% or higher. This is less then a half of the students.

False. Twelve students received a 70% or lower.

True. We know that the median score (the average of the 18th and 19th number) falls between 71% and 80% but we do not know the specific value.

2   **A**

A) True. The store carries 13 basketball and 5 climbing shoe types for a total of 18 types. This is greater than 15 types, the number of running shoe types.

B) False. The graph does not give any information about how much is sold.

C) False. The store has 9 types of walking shoes and 10 types of cross trainers and thus has more types of cross trainers than walking shoes.

D) False. The graph does not give any information about how much is sold.

3   **C**

A) False. The weights of Milo's fish have less variability as shown by the closeness of his data points.

B) False. The average weight of Jack's fish is $\frac{1.3 + 1.3 + 1.5 + 1.6 + 1.6 + 1.7 + 1.8 + 1.8}{8} = \frac{12.6}{8} = 1.575$ *pounds*. The average weight of Milo's fish is $\frac{1.2 + 1.2 + 1.2 + 1.5 + 1.7 + 1.8 + 2 + 2}{8} = \frac{12.6}{8} = 1.575$ *pounds*. Hence the average weights are the same.

C) True. Without any calculations you can see that Jacque's fish have weights farther away from the mean of 1.575 lbs than Milo's fish weight data.

D) False. Milo and Jacque caught the same weight in fish. See (B) above.

Question No.	Answer	Detailed Explanation

4

	10	14	17
Team 1: 15, 16, t, 17, 12, Mode = 17, What is t?			◉
Team 2: 7, 14, r, 16, 13 Mean = 12, What is r?	◉		
Team 3: 11, 7, 19, 14, z, Median = 14, What is z?		◉	

Team 1: t =12 would be the mode because it would be listed two times.

Team 2: (7 + 14 + r + 16 + 13) / 5 = 12
(50 + r) = 12 x 5 = 60
r = 60 - 50 = 10

Team 3: Arrange the known numbers in ascending order : 7, 11, 14, 19. It is given median is 14. Therefore, the unknown number z must be more than or equal to 14.
z = 14

5   **A**   The correct answer is A. Loving the smell of sea water supports loving the beach as far as a vacation trip. Although there are starfish in the ocean and sometimes aircraft fly by, neither of those details support the main idea of the paragraph. The author would not like vacationing at the beach if he/she hated the smell of sea water, so B is not correct.

6   **C**   The correct answer is C. Allison worked very hard and did not give up, and she eventually accomplished her goal. A is not correct because it will take people different amounts of time to accomplish what they set out to do. The key is to never give up. D is the opposite of what the passage is saying, and B is never mentioned.

Question No.	Answer	Detailed Explanations
7		Dear Mayor,

I know you are very busy, but there is an important issue I would like to address with you. The park in my neighborhood doesn't have enough tennis courts to accommodate all of the people who want to use them. Almost everyone in my neighborhood enjoys playing tennis, but there is only one court for all of us to share. This is a problem for many reasons.

First, most of us have to wait for hours to play tennis because there is only one court. This is inconvenient because we all try to come and play after school, and instead of getting to have some fun after school, we are waiting for hours to play one game. Tennis is a great way to keep kids active instead of them sitting on a couch and playing video games. Adding additional courts will help solve both these problems and keep the kids in your town active and healthy.

Next, the younger kids who want to play often have to go home before they even have the opportunity to get one game in. The parents enjoy knowing their kids are at the tennis courts and do not worry about them. However, if they continue having to wait so long, they may get bored and do something else, which may get them in trouble. Having a safe place for the kids to go is important. I know that the budget is tight this year, but I think that an additional tennis court would be a good investment for the neighborhood. Tennis is a great sport to play with friends and family. It helps keep us out of trouble by giving us something positive to do with our time. It helps keep us in shape and helps us learn friendly competition. When we play doubles, it also helps us learn to work in teams. If you are not able to add another tennis court at our park, I hope you will at least consider it. It would be good for our whole community.

Sincerely,
Tommy Brown
Grade 6

Question No.	Answer	Detailed Explanations
8	D	Answer choice D is correct. All of the statements about Christmas are positive, so this detail will be positive too. All of the other answer choices are negative.

Question No.	Answer	Detailed Explanation
1	D	To determine the number of goals he would need, Luis will need a total of 100 (20 * 5) goals. Set up an equation. Let x represent the goals needed for the 5th season: $14 + 15 + 18 + 21 + x = 100$ $72 + x = 100$ Subtract 72 from both sides. $72 + x - 72 = 100$ $x = 28$
2	B	Stacy would figure out the mode. The mode will tell her which heel height occurs most often when she lists them out.
3	A	To figure out the percentage, add together all of the ice cream cones sold by stand B. $24 + 8 + 14 = 46$ To find the percentage, divide 24 by 46 $24/46 = .522$ (when rounded to the nearest thousandth) To make the decimal into a percentage, move the decimal point to the right two places and round down. 52%

4

	5	10	20	25	30
0 – <5 cm		●			
5 – <10 cm	●				
10 – <15 cm		●			
15 – <20 cm			●		
20 – <25 cm					●

Question No.	Answer	Detailed Explanation
5	A	The passage is positive about younger siblings, so the answer choice will be positive. It is obvious that the author of the passage thinks that having younger siblings is great.
6	A	The correct answer is A. Because he spent all of the 5 dollars at the candy store, you can assume that he loves candy and did not think spending the money would be useless. That is the only answer that could be right. It never mentions what color his piggy bank is or sharing his candy.
7	B	The correct answer is B. It does not mention whether or not she has had her own room before or not. Her mother is not even mentioned and it said she was decorating her room pink, not purple.
8	A	Option A is the correct answer. Poet's purpose is stated throughout the small poem.

Question No.	Answer	Detailed Explanations
1	D	There are $(7+5+2) = 14$ players in all. The ratio of redheads to the team is 2:14. Divide by the GCF of 2 to simplify the ratio to 1:7
2	C	Set up the proportion: $\frac{2}{14} = \frac{x}{126}$, $\frac{1}{7} = \frac{x}{126}$, cross multiply to get $7x = 126$, then divide by 7 and $x = 18$.
3	D	The total number of birds is $175+63 = 238$. Thus, the ratio of ducks to total birds is 175:238. To find the ratio in simplest terms, divide by the GCF(175, 238) =7. The ratio in simplest terms is 25:34.

4		
1	2
2	4
3	6
4	8
5	10
6	12

The numbers are 3, 6, 10. The first row shows the ratio pattern, which is 1:2, which means each number in the left column is ½ of the number in the right column.

Question No.	Answer	Detailed Explanations
5	C	According to the passage, crabs and shrimp are crustaceans. That is specifically said in the passage.
6	A	An exoskeleton is a skeleton outside the body, so the answer is A.
7	B	Smelly has a negative connotation; fragrant is positive. Based on what the paragraph says, these smell good.
8	A	The only pair of opposite words is answer choice A.

Day 4

Question No.	Answer	Detailed Explanations
1	B	$7.55 x 10 = $75.55 $8.45 x 15 = $126.75 126.75 + 75.55 = 202.30 $$\frac{202.30}{25} = \$8.09$$
2	A	$\frac{15}{4} = \frac{60}{x}$, where 60 equals the number of minutes in an hour. 15 x 4 = 60, so multiply the original ratio $\frac{15}{4}$ by $\frac{4}{4}$ to get $\frac{60}{16}$, where 16 represents the miles per hour (mph) that she traveled.
3	C	Set up a ratio of distance/time. Here, the ratio would be $\frac{1.5}{2.5}$ Then, create a proportion $\frac{1.5}{2.5} = \frac{x}{60}$, where 60 represents the number of minutes in an hour. Find the cross products: 1.5*60 = 2.5*x Simplify: 90 = 2.5x, Divide each side by 2.5 we get, x = 36.

Question 4:

	1:10	1:5	1:50	1:20
$1.00 per 5 pounds		◯		
50 pounds per box			◯	
10 miles per gallon	◯			
1 lap in 20 minutes				◯

Correct Response: A. 1:5, One dollar is spent for every 5 pounds. B. 1:50, Per box refers to a quantity of 1 box, so there are 50 pounds in one box. C. 1:10, Per gallon refers to a quantity of 1 gallon, so every gallon supplies 10 miles. D. 1:20, It takes 20 minutes to run 1 lap.

Question No.	Answer	Detailed Explanations
5	C	The correct answer is C. The writer is writing in 1st person, and she is the main character in her story.
6	B	The correct answer is B. A major character will be a major part of the story. They will be in more of the story than minor characters.

Question No.	Answer	Detailed Explanations
7	A	Jane was very positive about starting a new school, so we are looking for a positive answer. They are all negative emotions except easy-going.
8	C	Greg was trying to see how things worked, not being mean to people. The answer choice is C. He was curious.

Question No.	Answer	Detailed Explanations
1	D	Since every foot = 12 inches, then 6 feet must equal 72 inches (6*12). Add extra 6 inches to 72 inches which is equal to 78 inches.
2	B	Divide a percentage by 100 to make an equivalent decimal form $7.5/100 = .075$
3	D	is/of = %/100 $$\frac{x}{60} = \frac{30}{100}$$ x*100 = 60*30 100x = 1800 Divide both sides by 100 x = $18 Subtract $18 from $60. $60−$18 = $42
4	A & C	A. $\frac{4}{6} = \frac{2}{3}$ & C. $\frac{6}{9} = \frac{2}{3}$ The ratio of grape to apple is 2:3 or $\frac{2}{3}$. By fractions equivalent to $\frac{2}{3}$, you can determine the correct ratio for the recipe.
5	B	Working like a dog means working really hard, so answer choice B is correct. This is a common saying.
6	A	Mules are known to be stubborn, so answer choice A is correct.
7	B	A mountain of work is a lot of work. Answer choice B is correct.
8	C	Quitting something cold turkey means that you quit suddenly and do it alone without any help.

STOP! IN THE NAME OF EDUCATION: PREVENT SUMMER LEARNING LOSS WITH 7 SIMPLE STEPS

Summer Learning loss is defined as "a loss of knowledge and skills . . . most commonly due to. . . . extended breaks [during the summertime] " (from edglossary.org/learning-loss). Many teachers have certainly had the experience of taking the first month of school not only to introduce his or her rules and procedures to the class but also to get the kids back "up to speed" with thinking, remembering what they've learned . . . and in many cases, reviewing previous content. With a traditional school calendar, then, this can mean that up to 10% of the school year is spent playing catch-up.

What's a parent to do? Fortunately, there are some simple steps you can take with your child to help your son or daughter both enjoy the summer and keep those all-important skills honed and fresh:

(1) Read!

Research supports the relationship between independent reading and student achievement, so simply having your child read daily will make a positive difference. Check out the following sources to find books that your child will want to dive into: your public library, local bookstores, online stores (Amazon, Barnes and Noble, half.com, etc.), and yard sales (if the family hosting the sale has children a bit older than your own, you stand a good chance of scoring discarded books that are a perfect match for your son or daughter's reading level).

(2) Write!

Have your child write letters to out-of-town friends and family, or write postcards while on vacation. A summer journal is another way to document summer activities. For the artistic or tech-savvy child, you may choose to create a family scrapbook with captions (consider the online options at Shutterfly, Mixbook, and Smilebox). Not only will you preserve this summer's memories, but your child will also continue to practice his or her writing skills! (See Summer is Here! Ideas to Keep Your Child's Writing Skills Sharp for more writing ideas.)

(3) Do the Math!

Think of ways your child can incorporate math skills into daily activities: have a yard sale, and put your child in charge of the cash box; help younger ones organize a lemonade stand (to practice salesmanship and making change). Or simply purchase a set of inexpensive flash cards to practice basic facts while waiting in line or on a long car ride. There's even a host of free online games that will keep your child's math skills sharp.

(4) "Homeschool" Your Child

Keeping your child's skills fresh doesn't have to cost a fortune: check out some of the Lumos Learning workbooks and online resources (at lumoslearning.com/store), and your child can work through several exercises each day. Even as little as twenty minutes a day can yield positive results, and it's easy to work in a small block of time here and there. For instance, your child can work in the book during a car ride, right before bedtime, etc. Or, simply make this part of your child's morning routine. For example: wake up, eat breakfast, complete chores, and then work in the workbook for 20 minutes. With time, you can make this a natural habit.

(5) Go Back-to-School Shopping (For a Great Summer School Learning Experience)

Check out offerings from the big names (think Sylvan, Huntington, Mathnasium, and Kumon), and also consider local summer schools. Some school districts and local colleges provide learning programs: research the offerings on-line for more information regarding the available options in your area.

(6) Take a Hike . . . Go Camping!

But "camp" doesn't always involve pitching a tent in the great outdoors. Nowadays, there are camps for every interest: sports camps, art camp, music camp, science camp, writing camp . . . the possibilities are endless! With a quick Internet search, you'll be able to turn up multiple options that will appeal to your son or daughter. And even if these camps aren't "academic", the life skills and interpersonal experiences are certain to help your child succeed in the "real world". For example, working together as a cast to put on a summer theater production involves memorizing lines, cooperation, stage crew coordination, and commitment – all skills that can come in handy when it comes to fostering a good work ethic and the ability to collaborate with others.

(7) Get tutored

Many teachers offer tutoring services throughout the summer months, either for individuals or small groups of students. Even the most school-averse student tends to enjoy the personal attention of a former teacher in a setting outside of the classroom. Plus, a tutor can tailor his or her instruction to pinpoint your child's needs – so you can maximize the tutoring sessions with the skills and concepts your child needs the most help with. Of course, you don't need to do all seven steps to ensure that your child maintains his or her skills. Just following through with one or two of these options will go a long way toward continued learning, skills maintenance, and easing the transition to school when summer draws to a close.

SUMMER READING: QUESTIONS TO ASK THAT PROMOTE COMPREHENSION

As mentioned in our "Beating Summer Academic Loss" article, students are at risk of losing academic ground during the summer months, especially with respect to their reading level, spelling, and vocabulary. One of the best ways to prevent this "brain drain" for literacy is to have your son or daughter read each day during the summer break.

Better yet, you can promote these all-important skills and participate in your child's summer reading by engaging in active dialogue with your son or daughter. Below are several questions and ideas for discussion that will promote comprehension, recall, and critical thinking skills. In addition, these questions reflect several of the Common Core standards – which underpin the curriculum, instruction and standardized testing for most school districts. Of course, the standards vary by grade level, but some of the common themes that emerge in these standards are: citing evidence, summarizing, and making inferences.

• Citing evidence

Simply put, citing evidence involves going back into the text (book, magazine, newspaper, etc.) and finding "proof" to back up an answer, opinion, or assertion. For instance, you could ask your child, "Did you enjoy this book?" and then follow up that "yes" or "no" response with a "Why?" This requires the reader to provide details and examples from the story to support his or her opinion. For this particular question, then, your child may highlight plot events he or she liked, character attributes, writing style, and even genre (type of book) as evidence. Challenge for older students: Ask your child to go back into the text and find a direct quote to support an opinion or answer.

• Summarizing

For nonfiction pieces, this may involve being able to explain the 5W's – who, what, where, when, why (and how). For literature, ask your child to summarize the story elements, including: the setting, characters, main conflict or problem, events, resolution, and theme/lesson/moral. If your child can do this with specificity and accuracy, there's a very good chance that he or she comprehended the story. Challenge for older students: Ask your child to identify more complex story elements, such as the climax, rising action, and falling action.

• Making inferences

Making an inference is commonly referred to as "reading between the lines." That is, the reader can't find the answer to a question directly in the text but instead must synthesize or analyze information to come to a conclusion. To enhance these higher-level thinking skills, ask your child to describe the main character's personality, describe how a character changed by the end of a novel, or detail how the setting influenced the story's plot. Challenge for older students: Have the reader compare and contrast two or more characters to highlight similarities and differences in personality, actions, etc.

Of course, if you read the same book that your child reads, you'll be able to come up with even more detailed questions – and also know if your child truly understood the reading based on his or her answers! But even if you don't get a chance to read what your child does, simply asking some of these questions not only helps your child's reading skills but also demonstrates an interest in your child – and his or her reading.

SUMMER IS HERE! KEEP YOUR CHILD'S WRITING SKILLS SHARP WITH ONLINE GAMES

Like Reading and math, free online activities exist for all subjects... and writing is no exception. Check out the following free interactive writing activities, puzzles, quizzes and games that reinforce writing skills and encourage creativity:

Primary Level (K-2nd Grade)

Story Writing Game

In this game, the child fills in the blanks of a short story. The challenge is for the storyteller to choose words that fit the kind of story that has been selected. For example, if the child chooses to tell a ghost story, then he or she must select words for each blank that would be appropriate for a scary tale. http://www.funenglishgames.com/writinggames/story.html

Opinions Quiz for Critical Thinking

Practice developing logical reasons to support a thesis with this interactive activity. Students read the stated opinion, such as, "We should have longer recess because..." The child must then select all of the possible reasons from a list that would support the given statement. The challenge lies

with the fact that each statement may have more than one possible answer, and to receive credit, the student must select all correct responses. This game is best suited for older primary students. http://www.netrover.com/~kingskid/Opinion/opinion.html

Interactives: Sequence

Allow your child to practice ordering events with this interactive version of the fairy tale, Cinderella. The child looks at several pictures from the story and must drag them to the bottom of the screen to put the events in chronological order. When the player mouses over each scene from the story, a sentence describing the image appears and is read aloud to the student. Once the events are in order, the student can learn more about the plot and other story elements with the accompanying tutorials and lessons. http://www.learner.org/interactives/story/sequence.html

BEATING THE BRAIN DRAIN THROUGH LITERACY: WEBINAR RECAP WITH PRINTABLE ACTIVITY SHEET

Lumos Learning conducted webinar on "Beating the Brain Drain Through Literacy." During this webinar, we provided the students with several ideas for keeping their literacy skills sharp in the summertime.

Here's a handy chart with the ideas from the webinar, ready for you to post on your refrigerator. Let your child pick and choose the activities that appeal to him or her. Of course, reading should be non-negotiable, but the list below provides alternatives for reluctant readers – or for those who just don't enjoy reading a traditional fiction novel. The first set of activities touch upon ideas that reinforce writing skills, while the second half addresses reading skills. There is also room on the chart to date or check off activities your child has completed.

Skill Area	Activity	Completed this activity	Notes for parents
Writing skills, spelling, and/or vocabulary	Keep a journal (things you do, places you go, people you meet)		Even though journals work on spelling skills, be sure your child understands that spelling "doesn't count". Most children like to keep their journals private, so they don't need to worry about perfect skills or that someone else is going to read/grade what they wrote.
	Start a blog		Enable privacy settings to keep viewers limited to friends and family. Check out WordPress, Squarespace, and Quillpad to begin blogging.
	Get published		The following places publish student work: The Clairmont Review, CyberKids, Creative Kids Magazine, New Moon, and The Young Writer's Magazine.
	Write letters		Have your child write or type letters, postcards, and emails to friends and family members.
	Take part in a family movie night		Watch movies that are thought-provoking to elicit interesting post-movie discussions. Other good bets are movies that are based on a book (read the book first and compare the two).
	Organize a family game night		Choose word games to work on spelling and vocabulary skills (examples: Scrabble, Boggle, and Hangman).
Reading skills: fluency, comprehension, critical thinking, decoding skills, inferencing, etc.	Pick up a good book!		Places to find/buy/borrow books include: your public library, ebooks, yard sales, book stores, your child's school library (if it's open during the summer), and borrowed books from friends and family members.

	Read materials that aren't "books"…		Ideas include: karaoke lyrics, cereal boxes, newspapers, magazines for kids, billboards, close captioning, and audio books.
	Compete! Enter a reading challenge		Scholastic Reading hosts a competition called "Reading Under the Stars" to break a world record for minutes read. Barnes and Noble gives students the opportunity to earn one free book with "Imagination's Destination" reading challenge.

Note: Reading just six books over the summer can maintain – and sometimes even increase! – your child's reading level. Not sure if the book is appropriate for your child's reading level? Use the five-finger rule: have your son/daughter read a page of a book. Each time your child encounters a word that is unfamiliar or unknown, he or she holds up a finger. If your child holds up more than five fingers on a given page, that book is probably too difficult.

However, there are some books that a child will successfully tackle if it's of high-interest to him or her. Keep in mind that reading levels are a guide (as is the five-finger rule), and some children may exceed expectations…so don't hold your child back if he or she really wants to read a particular book (even if it may appear to be too challenging).

Remember, if students do some of these simple activities, they can prevent the typical four to six weeks of learning loss due to the "summer slide." And since spelling, vocabulary and reading skills are vulnerable areas, be sure to encourage your child to maintain his or her current literacy level…it will go a long way come September!

WEBINAR "CLIFF NOTES" FOR BEATING SUMMER ACADEMIC LOSS: AN INFORMATIVE GUIDE TO PARENTS

The "Summer Slide"

First, it's important to understand the implications of "summer slide" – otherwise known as summer learning loss. Research has shown that some students who take standardized tests in the fall could have lost up to 4-6 weeks of learning each school year (when compared with test results from the previous spring). This means that teachers end up dedicating the first month of each new school year for reviewing material before they can move onto any new content and concepts.

The three areas that suffer most from summer learning loss are in the areas of vocabulary/reading, spelling, and math. In Stop! In the Name of Education: Prevent Summer Learning Loss With 7 Simple Steps, we discussed some activities parents could use with children to prevent summer slide. Let's add to that list with even more ways to keep children engaged and learning – all summer long.

Be sure to check out:

•Your Child's School

Talk to child's teacher, and tell him or her that you'd like to work on your child's academics over the summer. Most teachers will have many suggestions for you.

In addition to the classroom teacher as a resource, talk to the front office staff and guidance counselors. Reading lists and summer programs that are organized through the school district may be available for your family, and these staff members can usually point you in the right direction.

•Your Community

A quick Google search for "free activities for kids in (insert your town's name)" will yield results of possible educational experiences and opportunities in your area. Some towns offer "dollar days", park lunches, and local arts and entertainment.

You may even wish to involve your child in the research process to find fun, affordable memberships and discounts to use at area attractions. For New Jerseyans and Coloradans, check out www.funnewjersey.com and www.colorado.com for ideas.

Of course, don't forget your local library! In addition to books, you can borrow movies and audiobooks, check out the latest issue of your favorite magazine, and get free Internet access on the library's computers. Most libraries offer a plethora of other educational choices, too – from book clubs and author visits to movie nights and crafts classes, you're sure to find something at your local branch that your child will enjoy.

•Stores

This is an extremely engaging activity – and your child won't even know he or she is learning! For grocery shopping, ask your child to write the list while you dictate. At the store, your son/daughter can locate the items and keep a cost tally to stay within a specified budget. At the checkout, you can have a contest to see whose estimate of the final bill is most accurate – and then reward the winner!

You may wish to plan a home improvement project or plant a garden: for this, your child can make the list, research the necessary materials, and then plan and execute the project after a visit to your local home improvement store. All of these activities involve those three critical areas of spelling, vocabulary/reading, and math.

•The Kitchen

This is one of the best places to try new things – by researching new foods, recipes, and discussing healthy food choices – while practicing math skills (such as measuring ingredients, doubling recipes, etc.). Your child may also enjoy reading about new cultures and ethnicities and then trying out some new menu items from those cultures.

•The Television

TV doesn't have to be mind numbing ... when used appropriately. You can watch sports with your child to review stats and make predictions; watch documentaries; or tune into the History Channel, Discovery, National Geographic, HGTV, and more. Anything that teaches, helps your child discover new interests, and promotes learning new things together is fair game.

As an extension, you may decide to research whether or not the show portrays accurate information. And for those children who really get "into" a certain topic, you can enrich their learning by taking related trips to the museum, doing Internet research, and checking out books from the library that tie into the topic of interest.

•Movies

Movies can be educational, too, if you debrief with your child afterwards. Schedule a family movie

night, and then discuss how realistic the movie was, what the messages were, etc.

For book-based movies (such as Judy Moody, Harry Potter, Percy Jackson, etc.), you could read the book together first, and then view the movie version. Comparing and contrasting the two is another terrific educational way to enjoy time together and work on your child's reasoning skills.

Note: www.imdb.com and www.commonsensemedia.org are great sites for movie recommendations and movie reviews for kids and families.

•Games

Playing games promotes taking turns, reading and math skills, and strategy development. Scour yard sales for affordable board games like Scrabble, Monopoly, Uno, Battleship, and Qwirkle.

Don't forget about non-board games, like those found on the Wii, Nintendo, Xbox, and other gaming consoles. You'll still want to choose wisely and limit your child's screen time, but these electronic versions of popular (and new) games mirror the way kids think ... while focusing on reading and math skills. For more ideas, Google "education apps" for suggestions.

•Books, books, books!

Of course, nothing beats reading for maintaining skills. When you can connect your child with a book that is of interest to him or her, it can be fun for your child, build confidence, and improve fluency.

To help your child find a book that's "just right", use the five-finger rule: choose a page from a possible book and have your child read that page. Every time he or she encounters an unknown word, put up a finger. If your child exceeds five fingers (that is, five unknown words), that book is probably too challenging and he or she may wish to pass on it.

For reluctant readers, consider non-book reading options, like:magazines (such as Ranger Rick, American Girl, Discovery Kids, and Sports Illustrated for Kids), cereal boxes, billboards, current events, closed captioning, and karaoke. If you keep your eyes open, you'll find there are many natural reading opportunities that surround us every day.

Whatever you do, remember to keep it fun. Summer is a time for rest and rejuvenation, and learning doesn't always have to be scheduled. In fact, some of the most educational experiences are unplanned.

Visit lumoslearning.com/parents/summer-program for more information.

Valuable Learning Experiences: A Summer Activity Guide for Parents

Soon school will be out of session, leaving the summer free for adventure and relaxation. However, it's important to also use the summer for learning activities. Giving your son or daughter opportunities to keep learning can result in more maturity, self-growth, curiosity, and intelligence. Read on to learn some ways to make the most of this summer.

Read

Summer is the perfect time to get some extra reading accomplished. Youth can explore books about history, art, animals, and other interests, or they can read classic novels that have influenced people for decades. A lot of libraries have summer fun reading programs which give children, teens, and adults little weekly prizes for reading books. You can also offer a reward, like a $25 gift card, if your child reads a certain amount of books.

Travel

"The World is a book and those who do not travel read only a page." This quote by Saint Augustine illustrates why travel is so important for a student (and even you!). Travel opens our eyes to new cultures, experiences, and challenges. When you travel, you see commonalities and differences between cultures.

Professor Adam Galinsky of Columbia Business School, who has researched travel benefits, said in a Quartz article that travel can help a child develop compassion and empathy: "Engaging with another culture helps kids recognize that their own egocentric way of looking at the world is not the only way of being in the world."

If the student in your life constantly complains about not having the newest iPhone, how would they feel seeing a child in a third-world country with few possessions? If your child is disrespectful and self-centered, what would they learn going to Japan and seeing a culture that promotes respect and otherness instead of self-centeredness?

If you can't afford to travel to another country, start a family travel fund everyone can contribute to and in the meantime, travel somewhere new locally! Many people stay in the area they live instead of exploring. Research attractions in your state and nearby states to plan a short road trip to fun and educational places!

Visit Museums

You can always take your children to visit museums. Spending some quality time at a museum can enhance curiosity because children can learn new things, explore their interests, or see exhibits expanding upon school subjects they recently studied. Many museums have seasonal exhibits, so research special exhibits nearby. For example, "Titanic: The Artifact Exhibition" has been making its way to various museums in the United States. It contains items recovered from the Titanic as well as interactive activities and displays explaining the doomed ship's history and tragic demise. This year, the exhibit is visiting Las Vegas, Orlando, and Waco.

Work

A final learning suggestion for the summer is for students to get a job, internship, or volunteer position. Such jobs can help with exploring career options. For example, if your child is thinking of becoming a vet, they could walk dogs for neighbors, or if your child wants to start their own business, summer is the perfect time to make and sell products.

Not only will a job or volunteer work look good on college applications, but it will also teach your children valuable life lessons that can result in more maturity and responsibility. You could enhance the experience by teaching them accounting and illustrating real world problems to them, like budgeting money for savings and bills.

The above suggestions are just four of the many ways you can help learning continue for your child or children all summer long. Experience and seeing things first-hand are some of the most important ways that students can learn, so we hope you find the above suggestions helpful in designing a fun, educational, and rewarding summer that will have benefits in and out of the classroom.

What if I buy more than one Lumos Study Program?

Step 1

Visit the URL and login to your account.
http://www.lumoslearning.com

Step 2

Click on 'My tedBooks' under the "Account" tab.
Place the Book Access Code and submit.

Step 3

To add the new book for a registered student, choose the
○ Existing Student button and select the student and submit.

To add the new book for a new student, choose the ○ Add New student
button and complete the student registration.

Lumos StepUp® Mobile App FAQ For Students

What is the Lumos StepUp® App?

It is a FREE application you can download onto your Android Smartphones, tablets, iPhones, and iPads.

What are the Benefits of the StepUp® App?

This mobile application gives convenient access to Practice Tests, Common Core State Standards, Online Workbooks, and learning resources through your Smartphone and tablet computers.

- Eleven Technology enhanced question types in both MATH and ELA
- Sample questions for Arithmetic drills
- Standard specific sample questions
- Instant access to the Common Core State Standards
- Jokes and cartoons to make learning fun!

Do I Need the StepUp® App to Access Online Workbooks?

No, you can access Lumos StepUp® Online Workbooks through a personal computer. The StepUp® app simply enhances your learning experience and allows you to conveniently access StepUp® Online Workbooks and additional resources through your smartphone or tablet.

How can I Download the App?

Visit **lumoslearning.com/a/stepup-app** using your Smartphone or tablet and follow the instructions to download the app.

QR Code
for Smartphone
Or Tablet Users

Lumos StepUp® Mobile App FAQ
For Parents and Teachers

What is the Lumos StepUp® App?

It is a free app that teachers can use to easily access real-time student activity information as well as assign learning resources to students. Parents can also use it to easily access school-related information such as homework assigned by teachers and PTA meetings. It can be downloaded onto smartphones and tablets from popular App Stores.

What are the Benefits of the Lumos StepUp® App?

It provides convenient access to

- Standards aligned learning resources for your students
- An easy to use Dashboard
- Student progress reports
- Active and inactive students in your classroom
- Professional development information
- Educational Blogs

How can I Download the App?

Visit **lumoslearning.com/a/stepup-app** using your Smartphone or tablet and follow the instructions to download the app.

QR Code
for Smartphone
Or Tablet Users

Lumos tedBooks for State Assessments Practice

Lumos tedBook for standardized test practice provides necessary grade-specific state assessment practice and skills mastery. Each tedBook includes hundreds of standards-aligned practice questions and online summative assessments that mirror actual state tests.

The workbook provides students access to thousands of valuable learning resources such as worksheets, videos, apps, books, and much more.

Lumos Learning tedBooks for State Assessment	
SBAC Math & ELA Practice Book	CA, CT, DE, HI, ID, ME, MI, MN, NV, ND, OR, WA, WI
NJSLA Math & ELA Practice Book	NJ
ACT Aspire Math & ELA Practice Book	AL, AR
IAR Math & ELA Practice Book	IL
FSA Math & ELA Practice Book	FL
PARCC Math & ELA Practice Book	DC, NM
GMAS Math & ELA Practice Book	GA
NYST Math & ELA Practice Book	NY
ILEARN Math & ELA Practice Book	IN
LEAP Math & ELA Practice Book	LA
MAP Math & ELA Practice Book	MO
MAAP Math & ELA Practice Book	MS
AZM2 Math & ELA Practice Book	AZ
MCAP Math & ELA Practice Book	MD
OST Math & ELA Practice Book	OH
MCAS Math & ELA Practice Book	MA
CMAS Math & ELA Practice Book	CO
TN Ready Math & ELA Practice Book	TN

Available

- At Leading book stores
- www.lumoslearning.com/a/lumostedbooks